The
Year-Round
Gardener

The Year-Round Gardener

WARRINGTON BOROUGH COUNCIL	
Cypher	4.7.01
635.91	£14.99

Jane Courtier

MARSHALL PUBLISHING • LONDON

A Marshall Edition
Conceived by Marshall Editions Ltd
The Orangery
161 New Bond Street
London W1Y 9PA

Designed and edited by
Focus Publishing
The Courtyard
26 London Road
Sevenoaks
Kent TN13 3LJ

First published in the UK in 2001 by Marshall Publishing Ltd

ISBN 1 84028 388 2

Project Editor: Guy Croton
Editor: Gwen Rigby
Designer: Philip Clucas
Design Assistant: Sam Hemphill
Picture Researcher: Mel Watson
Indexer: Caroline Watson
Managing Editors: Antonia Cunningham, Judith Samuelson
Managing Art Editors: Philip Gilderdale, Patrick Carpenter
Editorial Director: Ellen Dupont
Art Director: Dave Goodman
Production Controller: Nikki Ingram, Anna Pauletti

Originated in Singapore by PICA Colour
Printed and bound in Portugal by Printer Portuguesa

Note: Measurements are given in metric and in imperial.
Follow one set or the other, since they are not interchangeable.

Jacket picture credits front and back:
TL Clive Nichols/Designer: Anthony Noel
TCL Harry Smith Collection
TCR Vaughan Fleming/The Garden Picture Library
TR Photos Horticultural Picture Library

Contents

Introduction

SEASONS IN THE GARDEN roll almost imperceptibly into one another. When snowdrops, winter aconites and early crocuses have been flowering for weeks, it is difficult to pinpoint the day when winter finally turns into spring; and when the first few scarlet and yellow leaves on the trees match the still-brilliant display of flowering border plants, who's to say if we have tipped over into autumn or whether it's still summer?

The seasons do matter, though, for if we are to get the most from our gardens there are tasks that need doing at certain times. With the busy lives most of us lead these days, it's only too easy to forget all those jobs we intended to do until it's too late.

I hope that this book will act as a memory jogger and problem solver, as well as an inspiration to try something new and different; also perhaps as a reminder of the delights each new gardening season has in store for us. Above all, we should try simply to enjoy our gardens, and not worry about them. If we don't get round to trying something this year, it's not the end of the world – there's always a new start to look forward to next spring!

Opposite Each of the seasons is epitomized by a specific image: cheerful daffodils in spring; voluptuous dahlias for summer; dazzling autumn leaves; and the winter miracle of the snowdrop.

How PLANTS GROW

You don't need to be a botanist or a scientist to grow good plants or to enjoy gardening, but a basic knowledge of how plants grow will certainly help you to get the best from your garden.

UNDERSTANDING plants' needs will mean that you are much more likely to be able to provide the right care for them. You will also have a better idea of what might be going wrong (and how to put it right) if they fail to thrive.

Photosynthesis Like all living things, plants need energy from food in order to survive. Plants have a distinct advantage over other life forms, however, in that they can obtain that energy from sunlight, which they convert into the carbohydrates they need by the process known as photosynthesis. This means that one of a plant's primary needs is light. It doesn't have to be sunlight – as long as it is of the correct intensity and wavelength, artificial light will do – but sunlight is the most common and usually most freely available source.

Light is not the only requirement for photosynthesis, however – the two other parts of the equation are water and carbon dioxide. Carbon dioxide is not a problem: it is freely available in the air and is something a gardener

Anemone japonica (Japanese anemone) is a vigorous plant that will thrive in a shady garden.

doesn't have to worry about. Water is different. As well as playing a vital part in food production, water is necessary for many other vital functions and forms some 90 per cent of a plant's tissues. Large quantities of water are lost by evaporation from leaves and other surfaces and need constant replacement. In natural conditions, plants have to rely on rainfall and dew to provide their water supply; in a garden, these are often supplemented by watering.

Essential nutrients Although light, air and water provide the raw materials for the manufacture of food, other chemicals are also necessary for plant growth and development. These chemicals include nitrogen, phosphorus and potassium; also essential are calcium, sulphur, magnesium, iron, and a range of other minerals. Other trace elements, or micronutrients, such as boron, copper, molybdenum, manganese and zinc, are also required in tiny amounts. All these nutrients are obtained from the soil, which is derived from broken-down rock and decaying plant and animal material. Sometimes the minerals are not present in sufficient quantities for the plants' needs, or they are not present in a form that is available to plants. Mineral deficiencies show up in a range of symptoms which a gardener can often recognize and correct by the application of fertilizers.

Introduction

Anatomy of a plant

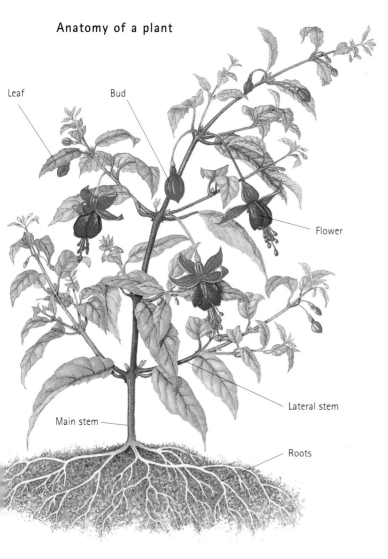

- Leaf
- Bud
- Flower
- Lateral stem
- Main stem
- Roots

Anatomy of a flower

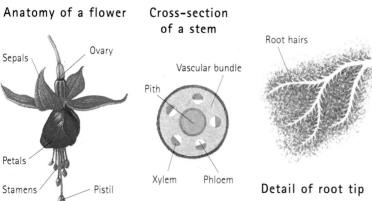

- Sepals
- Ovary
- Petals
- Stamens
- Pistil

Cross-section of a stem

- Pith
- Vascular bundle
- Xylem
- Phloem

- Root hairs

Detail of root tip

Temperature Another factor which is important to the growth of plants is the temperature of the surrounding air and the soil. Different species of plant thrive at different temperatures, but when the temperature goes beyond certain extremes growth slows dramatically and eventually stops. Overall, for most plants little growth occurs outside the range 5–25°C (40–77°F). The optimum range for plant growth tends to fall into roughly the temperature range at which humans also happen to function best – that is, around 10–20°C (50–70°F).

Outside the temperature range suitable for plant growth, some plants become dormant while others will die. The plants that are grown in our gardens are often not indigenous to the area or even the continent in which we grow them, and it is important for gardeners to know their likely response to seasonal temperature changes which may not occur in their natural habitat. Many plants originating from tropical areas, for example, can be grown successfully as summer bedding plants in northern climates, but will be killed outright at the first touch of frost (although sometimes the rootstock can remain dormant below the soil). Some of the more tender plants are treated as annuals in colder countries, while others will survive the winter if they are brought into a heated environment, such as a greenhouse, or a warm, bright room in the home.

The Importance of SOIL

The plant kingdom is astonishingly adaptable. Plants of some form or another are found in almost every region of the world.

THE PLANTS we grow in our gardens often have specific needs. Some are very exacting about the conditions in which they will grow, while others are far more easy-going.

Soil Nearly all plants grow in soil, which consists of rocks that have been eroded down to tiny particles over thousands of years plus the decaying remains of plants and animals, as well as a large population of living creatures. Soil provides essential water and minerals and also acts as a medium in which plants can anchor themselves.

The plants' anchor is their root system, which usually develops under-ground. Roots can take many different forms, but a typical plant has a spreading, branching root system which extends at least as widely as (usually more widely than) the growth above ground. Apart from securing the plant in the ground, roots also take up minerals and water from the soil. For this function, the most important parts are the tiny, fragile root hairs which grow a few millimetres back from the extreme tips of the roots (they can sometimes be seen on young

seedlings as a fluffy 'fuzz'). Because root hairs are so fragile they are easily damaged when a plant is pulled from the soil, which is why transplanting needs to be undertaken with great care. Root hairs can only take up liquids, so minerals must be dissolved in water before they can be used by the plants.

Soil is a very variable substance, differing in texture and chemical content from garden to garden as well as from

Make sure you use the correct compost when planting out or potting up. Soil-based compost contains most nutrients and retains water well – use it for shrubs and trees.

Peat-based compost is lighter to handle and cleaner but quickly runs out of nutrients and dries out easily – use it for annuals, bulbs and tubers.

Peat-substitute contains added nutrients and is good for plants such as chrysanthemums. Test its level of acidity before use.

Ericaceous compost contains no free lime – acid-loving plants such as heathers, azaleas and rhododendrons need it on order to thrive.

Light-weight compost containing water-retaining granules can be used to leaven manure and heavier materials.

one region to another. Gardeners can find out what type of soil they have by examining its feel and appearance and carrying out simple chemical tests.

The structure of the soil, as well as its chemical composition, is important for plant health. Soil should be 'friable' – broken down into fine crumbs – so that it can be penetrated easily by plant roots. The soil crumbs should be the right size so that they hold both air and water around them, since both are necessary for plant growth. Decayed organic matter (humus) is an essential constituent, acting as a sponge to retain moisture until it is needed by plants. The addition of suitable humus-forming materials is one way a gardener can greatly improve the condition of soil in the garden (see pages 156–157).

Soil itself is not essential for plant growth. Soilless culture, where plants grow with their roots bathed in a nutrient solution, is practised quite widely and is relatively popular for houseplants, although it is not usually practical in a garden situation. Greater numbers of gardens, however, have a limited amount of natural soil as the use of labour-saving paving and other surfacing materials increases. Plants in paved gardens may be grown in containers such as tubs, troughs and hanging baskets, and the most popular growing medium used to fill these is manufactured compost.

The Plant ENVIRONMENT

Climate obviously has a significant effect on plant growth, since it determines major factors such as extremes of temperature, hours of sunshine and amount of rainfall received by the plants.

THE CLIMATE varies from continent to continent, country to country and region to region, but a surprisingly wide range of different conditions can be experienced by plants even within the same small garden. An area of flowerbed under the permanent shade of an evergreen tree may remain cool, dark and damp, while a few yards away, plants growing out in the full sun at the base of a sheltering wall will be experiencing very hot, dry, bright conditions. The effects of these 'micro-climates' are just as important to take into account as the larger climate picture.

Light and shade The majority of plants grow best in bright conditions, where they receive maximum light for photosynthesis. Plants growing in shady positions may develop thin, pale, soft growth as they struggle to reach the light; variegated or coloured leaves often revert to plain green in an attempt to photosynthesise more efficiently in low light levels. Some plants, however, are better adapted than others to shady conditions, since they grow naturally under a woodland canopy. Hellebores, violets, hostas, ivy and periwinkle are all naturally adapted to low light conditions.

In the garden, shade can be caused by overhanging trees, hedges and fences, walls and buildings. It may be deep and permanent or light and dappled, sometimes occurring only during certain seasons or times of day. Where the amount of shade is significant and cannot be reduced, shade-tolerant plants should be selected.

Water
Gardeners tend to associate shortage of water with hot, sunny conditions, but this is not always the case. Sunshine and heat certainly increase the amount of evaporation from soil and plant tissues, and can lead to rapid wilting if the water is not replaced. But evaporation is also increased by wind, and plants can easily be damaged by water stress in cool, dull, windy conditions. Shady areas are often cool and damp, but where the shade is caused by overhanging trees, the soil may in fact be very dry – the tree roots take huge quantities of water from the

soil while the dense foliage canopy prevents rain replenishing it.

Plants that are adapted to dry conditions often have grey or silver foliage (to reflect intense light) which is very narrow or needle shaped to cut down unnecessary evaporation. Leaves may be covered with fine hairs to reduce water loss further. *Artemisia* (wormwood), *Cistus* (sun rose), lavender, rosemary, *Phlomis* (Jerusalem sage) and *Santolina* (cotton lavender) are typical of the sort of plants that do well in hot, dry, sunny positions.

Wind Those gardeners who have very exposed and windy gardens soon come to appreciate the damage that it can cause. Apart from occasional instances when large trees are uprooted in gale conditions, there are many far less dramatic instances of wind damage. Wind accelerates the evaporation of water from plants, and plants in exposed positions soon develop brown margins to their foliage. Young growths and buds can be killed by drying winds, as is often clearly shown by the stunted, one-sided development of trees in open, windswept landscapes. Strong winds are more

Alpines – those plants that in the wild grow above the tree line – are good plants for dry, exposed areas, since their spreading root systems enable them to find nutrients in poor, stony soil, and their low growth habit helps them to resist the wind. They will even do well in shallow terracotta pots, provided they are planted in free-draining soil and the crowns protected from waterlogging, or they will rot and die.

LIVING WITH A LARGE TREE
The branches of a large tree cast a wide shadow, and, if they are shallow, the roots will deplete the soil over a wide area, with the result that the soil will be dry and in permanent shade. Turn this into an asset by making a paved sitting-out place beneath the tree, and planting ferns, hellebores and some geraniums and euphorbias, which can tolerate deep shade. In summer, bring in some colourful and sweet-scented plants in pots for short spells to lighten the ambience.

common in coastal gardens, and may also be laden with salt, which can be particularly damaging.

Providing an efficient shelter against the wind is an important aspect of getting plants established in an exposed garden, whether the shelter consists of a large-scale shelter belt of shrubs, or temporary, individual windbreaks for newly planted specimens. More detail on protecting plants from the effects of wind can be found on pages 174–175.

TOOLS *and* EQUIPMENT

Gardening is like many other hobbies – there are almost endless gadgets and pieces of equipment you can buy if you feel so inclined. However, the list of essential equipment for a garden is actually fairly short.

THE TOOLS you will need depend to some extent on the size and type of garden you have and the type of plants you intend to grow in it, but the following are likely to be among the most useful.

Fork and spade You will need these if you have any open areas of soil in which to grow plants. Light, free-draining soils are easier to turn over, and here you may be able to get away with just a garden fork, but for heavier soils and larger expanses (such as a vegetable plot) you will need a digging spade as well. Make sure that the tools are comfortable to handle and an appropriate size; longer-handled tools are often a good bet since they provide extra leverage. Stainless steel tools have a long life and are easy to clean and care for, if you can afford the higher price.

Trowel Essential for all planting jobs, including planting in containers. The trowel should be strongly made (check that the joint between blade and handle will not bend in firm soil) and have a comfortable handle which does not irritate the heel or palm of your hand when it is being used.

Rake A garden rake is used to level and break down the soil into fine crumbs when seed-sowing, while for gathering up leaves and clippings, a spring-tine rake is the most useful.

Hoe A Dutch hoe, with a flat blade, is excellent for dealing with seedling

weeds in flower or vegetable beds. The blade should be kept very sharp, so the weeds are sliced off at soil level – a hoe

Introduction

is not intended to be used for digging weed seedlings out of the soil, but for skimming across the soil surface.

Secateurs and shears Secateurs are needed for pruning jobs, while shears are useful for trimming hedges, lawn edges and long grass. Check that

The tools you need will depend to some extent on the size and type of garden you have

secateurs are comfortable to hold, with an easily operated safety catch, and be especially careful that they do not pinch your hand as they close. Whether you choose anvil or cross-bill type of blades is a matter of personal preference. If you do not have a strong grip, you may find ratchet secateurs useful – these cut large stems with a minimum of effort. Shears should also be comfortable to use, with smoothly operating blades. For trimming lawn edges, use long-handled edging shears.

Watering can and hose A watering can fitted with a fine rose on the end of the spout is useful for watering trays of

seedlings and young plants, as well as plants in containers. For anything but a very small garden, a hose will be a time saver, allowing efficient and easy watering of beds, borders and lawns; a variety of hose-end fittings will enable you to obtain a spray or jet of water. For watering large areas, a sprinkler is valuable, although its use may require a licence or water meter in some areas.

Lawn mower and hedge trimmer For small, 'pocket handkerchief' lawns, a hand push mower may be sufficient, but for medium-sized and large lawns a power mower requires far less effort. Choose from electric or petrol models; rotary mowers are the most versatile, while cylinder mowers traditionally give the finest cut.

Hand shears may be sufficient for clipping small, low hedges, but powered trimmers make lighter work of a tiresome chore. Make sure a trimmer is strong enough for the job; some cheaper models are meant only for light clipping of soft growth and will be easily damaged if used for anything remotely heavy duty. Always treat all power tools with respect, observing manufacturers' safety precautions and wearing suitable protective clothing and gloves when necessary. Be especially careful with electrical equipment out of doors; never use it in wet weather and acquire a residual current device to attach to the equipment to avoid potentially fatal electric shocks.

The range of essential garden tools is surprisingly small and relatively inexpensive these days.

Clockwise from top left: Tulips and myosotis; spring border; mixed rhododendrons; mixed crocus naturalized in grass; camellia; bluebells and ferns.

Spring

INSPECTION

Spring must be every gardener's favourite season of the year. Winter is over at last, plants are starting into growth, days are lengthening and the garden is filled with birdsong from dawn to dusk. Who could fail to feel optimistic at such a time?

After the first few tentative signs of spring, the season soon seems to be falling over itself in its sudden, headlong rush into growth. For gardeners, spring is perhaps the busiest season of all. There are flowers and vegetables to be sown, shrubs to prune, lawns to mow. Weeds appear and grow faster and stronger than any cultivated plant, and pests join the general throng of insect life, threatening to demolish all the progress our plants have made. There's plenty to do in the garden, but there's plenty to enjoy, too. Among all your tasks, make time to stand and appreciate the sights, scents and sounds around you.

SPRING CHECKLIST

Spring

☑ Divide overcrowded clumps of herbaceous border plants and replant young sections.

☑ Check all plants for evidence of pests and diseases. Early treatment often prevents major problems developing.

☑ Mulch moist, weed-free soil in beds and borders to help retain moisture through the summer months.

☑ Finish digging the vegetable garden and break the soil down to fine crumbs for seed sowing.

☑ Sow hardy annuals where they are to grow in flowerbeds outdoors.

☑ Take softwood cuttings of greenhouse plants such as pelargoniums and chrysanthemums.

☑ Begin to mow lawns, keeping the blades high for the first few cuts. Feed lawns with a spring fertilizer.

☑ When spring bulbs cease flowering, allow the leaves to die down naturally. This builds up the bulbs for a good display next year.

☑ Sow vegetables for a succession of crops. Sow tender vegetables in pots under cover; plant out after the risk of frost is over.

☑ Thin out established pond plants. Introduce new fish to ponds.

☑ Trim evergreen hedges, cutting the bases slightly wider than the top to give a wedge shape.

☑ Thin out seedlings planted earlier, leaving the strongest plants.

Sowing ANNUALS

Annual flowers are those that grow from seed, flower, set seed themselves and then die, all within a year. They are a cheap and relatively easy way to provide some attractive colour in the garden, and there are many different varieties to choose from.

Mark out areas with sand when sowing annuals directly in the border, and sow in straight lines.

Lobularia maritima (syn. *Alyssum maritimum*) (sweet alyssum) needs sunlight and well-drained soil to prosper. The plants should be cut back lightly after flowering.

ANNUALS ARE split into two groups – hardy and half-hardy. Hardy annuals are those that will withstand a fair degree of cold and can be sown outdoors where they are to grow in early spring. Some varieties can even be sown in autumn, to overwinter outside and provide a specially early show of flowers. Half-hardy annuals are more sensitive to cold. Many are best raised in pots and trays under cover in a greenhouse or conservatory, but some can also be sown outdoors in mid- to late spring, when the danger of frost damaging the seedlings should be over.

Annuals are best grown in groups in the border. The soil should first be dug over and broken down to fine crumbs, with an application of general fertilizer raked into the surface. Positions for the groups of annuals can then be marked out with a stick or trickle of sand, dividing the soil into overlapping segments. Within each segment, sow a thin trickle of one variety of seed in shallow, parallel rows. Don't be tempted to scatter the seed randomly over the whole segment, or it will be impossible to sort out weed seedlings from the annuals when they start to germinate. To prevent too much of a regimented look, alter the direction of the rows in adjoining segments.

Note the eventual height of the annual varieties from the seed packets, and arrange the sowings so that the

shortest varieties are positioned at the front of the border and the tallest at the back. If a whole bed is to be devoted to annuals, it is worth spending a little time drawing out a plan before sowing. Take into account the height, season, colour and texture of the flowers, positioning them as appropriate to achieve the best effect.

As soon as the seeds are sown, cover them lightly with soil and firm it gently. If watering is necessary, it should be done through a fine rose to avoid washing the seeds out of the drills.

As the seedlings germinate, the annuals will appear in straight rows. There are likely to be plenty of weed seeds germinating, too; remove these by hand. Once the annual seedlings have developed sufficiently, thin them out in stages to leave plants at a final spacing of between 10 and 30cm (4–12in), depending on variety.

Centaurea cyanus (cornflower) is a strong, erect plant that thrives in any well-drained soil. Both tall and dwarf varieties are widely available.

Hardy annuals to sow in early spring
*Lobularia (*syn. *Alyssum)* (sweet alyssum)
Calendula (pot marigold)
Centaurea (cornflower)
Consolida (larkspur)
Eschscholzia (Californian poppy)
Limnanthes (poached egg plant)
Matthiola bicornis (night-scented stock)
Nigella (love-in-a-mist)

Half-hardy annuals to sow after frost
Ageratum (floss flower)
Antirrhinum (snapdragon)
Callistephus (china aster)
Impatiens (busy lizzie)
Lobelia
Nicotiana (tobacco plant)
Petunia
Salvia
Tagetes (french marigold)
Zinnia

Tagetes 'Tangerine Gem' creates a glowing carpet of orange that contrasts well with more muted colours.

Zinnia angustifolia provides varied colours and bold seedheads and is excellent for cutting.

Limnanthes douglasii (poached egg plant) is an erect, fast-growing annual with shiny, finely cut leaves and scented, cup-shaped flowers.

Brachycome iberidifolia (Swan River daisy) is an ideal plant for container growing, with daisy-like flowers and fine, ferny, light green foliage.

Care of BORDER PLANTS

The perennial Geranium 'Johnson's Blue' provides a splash of intense colour in the border.

however, strong new shoots come thrusting through the soil to remind us of their continued presence, and it is at this early stage of growth that a little work can help to ensure a good show of flowers.

Tidying crowns Any dead stems and leaves that have remained on the crowns over winter should now be cleared away, taking care not to damage the new young shoots. Weeds should also be removed.

Slug damage The juicy young shoots of herbaceous perennials provide a favourite snack for slugs and snails. Clear away plant debris, which could shelter the pests, and deter them by encircling particularly vulnerable plants with sharp grit. Slug traps or biological control using a nematode can keep slug

As long as we look after them well, we can rely on border plants to provide a fine display of summer colour in gardens for year after year.

THE TERM 'border plants' generally means herbaceous perennials – plants that die down completely each autumn but regrow from below ground every spring. Among old favourites are lupins, delphiniums, asters, campanulas, peonies and many others.

Because their top growth dies away, it is easy to forget that border plants are still there through the winter months. In early to mid-spring,

Because their top growth dies away, it is easy to forget that border plants are still there through the winter months

rejuvenated by division. Autumn is probably the best time to do this job (see pages 116–117).

Taking cuttings If you have a perennial plant you are particularly keen to increase, you can take advantage of the number of new shoots it produces in spring to propagate it. When the young shoots are about 10cm (4in) high, cut off several of them as close as possible to their base with a sharp knife. Pot them up in moist, soilless compost and cover them with a plastic propagator cover. Keep them in a sheltered position, out of direct sun, and they should form roots within a few weeks. Do not take more than about one-third of the total shoots produced by the crown as cuttings, to avoid spoiling the flower display.

Providing support Tall border plants need support if they are not to be damaged by rain and wind, and these supports should be provided as soon as the shoots start to grow. Getting the supports in place early will enable the plants to keep in shape throughout the season. If they are left until late spring or early summer, it is almost impossible to achieve a natural-looking effect. Twiggy sticks, strategically placed canes and twine, wire mesh and purpose-made supports of various designs can all be used successfully. Train the plants into the supports carefully as they grow.

WIGWAM OF CANES
A wigwam made of canes of about 2.4m (8ft) in length makes an excellent support for fast-growing climbers such as sweet peas. The structure allows air to circulate and provides plenty of room for the plants to spread outwards and upwards.

numbers down, or as a last resort they can be killed with slug bait if you have no objection to using it. Make sure slug pellets are not accessible to wild birds and animals or domestic pets.

Division After three or four years, the crowns of many border plants will have formed a large clump, often with a bare, dead centre. These plants can be

It is often necessary to provide support for individual stems rather than for the plant as a whole, but avoid trussing up the stems too tightly.

A metal framework supports a plant without twine or tying. The stems are held fairly freely, so they can grow through the frame and bend but not flop.

Summer-flowering BULBS

Everyone knows that spring is the season when bulbs come into their own, but fewer gardeners realize how many attractive summer-flowering bulbous plants there are. Many of these are rather tender, and are planted out in mid- to late spring, when frost will no longer threaten the young shoots as they come through the soil.

BULBOUS PLANTS give a wonderful display of blooms through the summer months, with some of them extending their flowering period until well into the autumn.

Most summer-flowering bulbs like a sheltered, sunny site and light, free-draining soil: heavy soil and damp conditions can cause the bulbs to rot. Unless the soil is very light, add some coarse sand or grit to the planting area, digging it in along with an application of general fertilizer. If the weather has been very wet around planting time, sprinkle a little sand in the bottom of each planting hole before dropping in the bulb, to ensure that the base of the bulb is not sitting in water.

The following list of summer-flowering plants should strictly be referred to as bulbous plants, since they are not all true bulbs but include tubers, corms and rhizomes as well.

Anemone coronaria will flower almost all year round if corms are planted in succession.

Poppy-flowered anemone
Anemone coronaria
Produces large, bright, cup-shaped flowers with dark centres. Plant in early spring for flowers from midsummer on.

Gladioli, with their strong, erect stems, form an effective backdrop for other border plants. Hybrids are available in a wide range of colours.

Swamp lily *Crinum powellii*
Tall, sturdy flower spikes carry large, trumpet-shaped, sweet-scented white or pink flowers in late summer and early autumn. Plant in a sheltered position in mid- to late spring and protect the bulbs with bark mulch over winter.

Montbretia *Crocosmia crocosmiiflora*
Wiry spikes of brightly coloured red, orange or yellow star-like flowers from midsummer to early autumn. Plant in early to mid-spring; in cold areas, mulch with shredded bark over winter.

Pineapple flower *Eucomis autumnalis, E. bicolor, E. comosa*
Rosettes of leaves produce strong flower stems with dense spikes of white or greenish, lily-like flowers topped with a tuft of leaves which give the plant its common name. Suitable for mild areas. Plant in early to mid-spring.

Sword lily *Gladiolus* hybrids
Tall, stiff spikes of open, trumpet-shaped flowers in a very wide range of colours. Plant from early to late spring; stake the flowering stems.

Acidanthera *Gladiolus callinathus*
White, asymmetric flowers with a central purple-brown blotch and a lovely, sweet scent. Plant mid-spring for flowers in late summer and early autumn. Lift corms after flowering, dry and store over winter.

Guernsey lily *Nerine bowdenii*
Rounded heads of up to a dozen trumpet-shaped flowers, rather like a low-growing pink agapanthus. Late flowering, from late summer to mid-autumn. Plant in mid-spring.

Peacock flower, tiger flower
Tigridia pavonia
Very showy, with three large outer petals and three small inner petals which are usually strikingly splashed and blotched with bright colours. Bulbs are best lifted in autumn and overwintered under cover. Plant in late spring.

Tall, hardy *Lilium henryi* bears pale yellow flowers. Plant bulbs from autumn to early spring.

To propagate lilies from relatively immature bulbs, remove single scales and press them into seed compost, tip uppermost. They should flower in 3–4 years.

Some lilies produce bulbils on the stem. Remove them after the flowers have faded and press them into seed compost, with their tips just below the surface. They should flower in 3–4 years.

Clumps of mature lilies may be lifted in autumn and divided by hand. Be careful not to damage the bulbs as you pull them apart.

Preparing CONTAINERS

Flowering plants in containers are suitable for all types of garden. Containers have many plus points: they are quick and easy to plant up and simple to colour-theme; they provide bright 'accents' of colour wherever it is needed, and they can usually be moved around the garden if desired.

ALTHOUGH THEY are so adaptable, it is a mistake to plant containers up too early. Bedding plants are available in garden centres from very early spring, and it is tempting to buy them while there is still a good selection. However, most of the plants available would be severely damaged or killed by a late spring frost, so planted containers should never be put outdoors until all danger of frost has passed. If you have a heated greenhouse, you can buy plants in early spring and grow them on in there, ready for setting out later; otherwise, hold fire until you are sure that it is safe.

However, early spring is not too soon to start planning, and preparing the containers for planting. The range of containers available is very large; ground-based types include pots, tubs and troughs of various shapes and sizes and manufactured from a variety of materials such as plastic, stone or wood. It is usually best to choose a material and design that blends well

SPACE AND DRAINAGE
Choose the right-sized container for the plant and make sure that the drainage is good. Plastic pots have drainage holes around the outside edge; clay pots have a single central hole.

Pots and containers come in a huge variety of materials, sizes, shapes and styles. Bear in mind that large containers will always be difficult to move around the garden, so a selection of smaller ones might be a more favourable option.

with the style of house and garden, although a deliberate contrast can also be very effective.

Window boxes, wall pots and hanging baskets allow a three-dimensional effect to be obtained, making use of walls and fences surrounding the garden as well as house walls. Pergolas, sheds, arches and other garden structures can also support planted containers.

If you intend to reuse containers you already have, these should be cleaned up now. Any soil and plant remains still in them should be disposed of, and the inside and outside of the container thoroughly cleaned with warm water

Choose a *material* and *design* that blend well with the style of house and garden

containing a little garden disinfectant. It is the inside of the container that is the most important, since disease-causing organisms may persist in traces of old plants and soil and could infect new plants.

Once the containers have been cleaned, ensure that you have materials such as crocks to place over drainage holes to ensure free drainage, plenty of suitable compost, some slow-release fertilizer, water-retaining granules, and hanging basket liners. Containers need plenty of watering during the summer, so check that watering cans, hoses and fittings are all in good condition, and replace them where necessary.

Finally, think about colour schemes or particular plants that you would like to include in the containers this year, perhaps writing down ideas before you buy the plants. Also, jot down the number and size of containers that you need to fill so that you will be better able to estimate the number of plants you need to buy.

Hanging baskets are wonderfully versatile plant containers that can be hung just about anywhere for instant decorative effects.

Bowls come in many different materials and colours and make useful and attractive plant containers for both indoors and outdoors.

Barrels and tubs make stylish, long-lasting containers that provide a good home to many different types of plant.

Pruning TREES AND SHRUBS

Pruning can be a great worry to many gardeners, who are never quite sure of the right time or way to prune shrubs and trees – or even whether they need to be pruned at all. However, it need not be so daunting or mysterious.

Keep *Potentilla fruticosa* bushy and vigorous by cutting out weak or old stems at ground level.

Prune established plants of *Tamarisk pentandra* in early spring, removing half to two-thirds of the previous season's growth to keep the plants bushy.

THERE ARE several objectives in pruning. First is to maintain an attractive shape to the plant and prevent it outgrowing its allotted space; second is to remove dead, unhealthy or non-typical growth; and third is to encourage the maximum production of flowers or of flowers and fruit. Pruning at the wrong time or in the wrong way can certainly spoil the flowering potential and perhaps the shape of a plant, but it is unlikely to have a lasting effect, and can usually be put right within a year or two, so there is no need to worry too much about it.

The types of ornamental trees and shrubs which are pruned in early spring – just before or as they are about to start into growth – are deciduous varieties that flower in summer. They bear their flowers on new growth which has been produced that year, so cutting

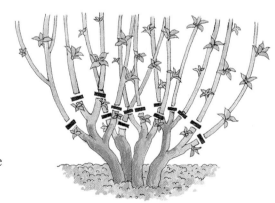

BASIC PRUNING
Cut the stems of plants such as *Cornus stolonifera* and *Eucalyptus gunnii* to within a hand's breadth of the ground to promote attractive young shoots.

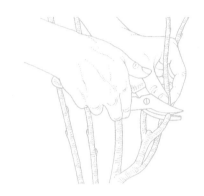

PRUNING YOUNG PLANTS
Prune young plants very lightly. Remove only unwanted growth that disturbs the shape. This is usually unnecessary on more mature shrubs.

ENCOURAGING NEW GROWTH
Cut back old and dying stems after flowering to allow new growth to flourish, so encouraging profuse flowering the following season.

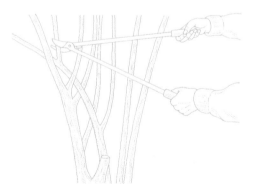

HARD PRUNING
Use long-handled secateurs to cut back thicker, woody stems. Leave a few strong buds on shrubs that flower on the current season's growth.

plants back in late winter and early spring will promote the maximum amount of strong young shoots with flowering potential.

The techniques of pruning are not difficult. A sharp pair of secateurs is the first essential; blunt blades will leave a ragged cut that is more prone to disease attack, and they also make pruning much harder work.

Where possible, pruning cuts should be made just above an outward-pointing bud, leaving a surface that slopes away slightly from the bud.

The first step when pruning a tree or shrub is to cut out obviously dead wood, then all diseased or damaged wood. This always has to be removed, no matter what sort of plant is being pruned.

Many shrubs that are pruned at this time of year are easy – they can be cut back very hard, almost to ground level; the shape of the whole plant will then be formed by the new growths.

Shrubs and trees to prune in spring
Buddleja davidii (butterfly bush)
Ceanothus (Californian lilac)
Ceratostigma willmottianum (hardy plumbago, leadwort)
Cornus alba (dogwood)
Fuchsia – hardy varieties
Hibiscus syriacus
Hydrangea paniculata
Potentilla fruticosa (shrubby cinquefoil)
Spiraea douglasii
Tamarix pentandra (tamarisk)

Lavatera 'Barnsley' (tree mallow) is a good example of a shrub that requires pruning in spring, when damaged or dead stems should be cut out. It bears glossy-petalled flowers on tall stems that need staking.

Clerodendrum trichotomum is a large shrub with fragrant flowers followed by blue berries. It benefits from a tidy-up in spring. Any frost-damaged shoot tips should be cut off, and large woody plants can be cut back to about 30cm (12in) from the ground.

Pruning ROSES

The ideal time to prune roses is early to mid-spring. In spring it is easy to see the healthy, swelling buds on the stems, so pruning cuts can be made in just the right place. Once the stem has been cut back, the buds grow away with increased vigour.

A good rose garden can offer all the colour, form and fragrance that a gardener could want.

THE MOST POPULAR roses for gardens are the large- and cluster-flowered bushes. These used to be called hybrid tea and floribunda roses respectively, and many gardeners still refer to them by the old names. They produce their best flowers on new shoots, so they are pruned quite hard each year to stimulate shoot production.

There are two main methods of pruning roses; the traditional method and a more modern one which is very simple and gives surprisingly good results.

Traditional pruning The traditional method starts, as with all pruning, by removing dead, damaged and diseased shoots. Cut these right back into healthy growth, until the centres of the cut branches show no signs of a brown stain in the tissue. Next, cut out any very thin or weak shoots that may be present.

Rosa 'Sexy Rexy' is an abundant cluster-flowered rose with an upright habit and light pink flowers.

The most popular roses for gardens are the

Hard pruning stimulates strong growth, so weak-growing roses should be pruned harder than strong, vigorous ones. The main stems of the rose can be cut back to within two or three buds of the base, though most are pruned rather less severely, leaving around 20–30cm (8–12in) of stem above ground. Hard pruning produces fewer, but higher-quality blooms.

The centre of a rose bush should be kept 'open'. When pruning, therefore, select an outward-pointing bud to cut, as this will produce an outward-growing stem. Shoots which are growing into the centre of the bush should generally be removed.

Modern pruning This method was developed from trials carried out by the Royal National Rose Society. Instead of selecting individual stems and pruning to just above an outward-facing bud, rose bushes were simply cut to half their height, using a powered hedge trimmer. Surprisingly, the results obtained compared very well with roses pruned by the traditional methods, with good numbers of high-quality blooms. Despite the fact that weak, twiggy, inward-growing stems were left on the bushes, there seemed to be no greater problem with disease, and the time taken over pruning on a large scale was obviously hugely reduced.

Rosa 'Madame Butterfly' is a good example of an early large-flowered rose that should be judiciously pruned in late winter or early spring.

Rosa 'Allgold' is a vigorous, disease-resistant cluster-flowered rose that should be cut back in early spring.

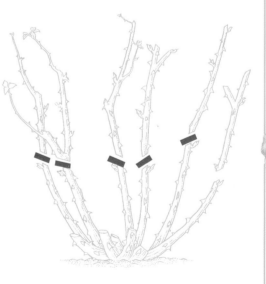

PRUNING CLUSTER-FLOWERED ROSES
In early spring, cut back dead and dying wood to the base of the plant. Then cut back the shoots that remain, shortening them by about a third.

PRUNING LARGE-FLOWERED ROSES
Prune in very early spring. Cut back weak stems to the base and then remaining shoots by about half their length. On a weak plant, remove a little more.

Rosa 'Queen Elizabeth' forms a large upright bush. This is a good example of a cluster-flowered rose that might require heavier pruning.

large- and cluster-flowered bushes

Care of TREES AND SHRUBS

The leaves of slow-growing *Acer pseudoplatanus* 'Brilliantissimum' are shrimp-pink in spring.

Trees and shrubs give a long season of value in the garden, but they are sometimes rather neglected. They can often be improved by a little regular attention.

IN SPRING, as the leaves of deciduous varieties are starting to open, it is easy to spot any dead branches that may be present, and these should be pruned out as soon as they are noticed, cutting right back into healthy wood. Clear away weeds that are growing beneath the plants, and check that the soil is moist. In free-draining soils, watering is often necessary during the late spring and summer, particularly in the early years after planting. Soil which appears moist on the surface can often be quite dry farther down, by the roots. On light soils and in dry areas, it is a good idea to sink a vertical length of pipe close to the tree, preferably when planting; then, when water is required it can be applied through the pipe so that you can be sure it is reaching the roots.

Once established, trees and shrubs tend to be left to fend for themselves

Many trees and shrubs will benefit from an application of fertilizer in spring, though this is not always necessary. Varieties that are grown for their flowers or fruits should be given a fertilizer high in potash; for others, use a balanced, general fertilizer. Vigorous plants, which may be in danger of outgrowing their space, do not need to be fertilized as long as they are making healthy growth. In small to medium-sized

Berberis darwinii (Darwin's barberry) has a profusion of deep orange-yellow flowers from the middle to the end of spring.

A dribble bar attached to a watering can, as shown here, offers an easily controllable way to apply weedkiller to grass growing around shrubs and young trees.

Dig out any stubborn, deeply rooted weeds with a hand fork. Then water and apply fertilizer and a mulch to encourage vigorous, healthy growth.

Small, delicate trees such as this pretty flowering almond (*Prunus* x *amygdalopersica* 'Pollardii') need particular care and attention.

gardens, it is often necessary to slow down the growth of trees rather than encourage it; grassing up to the trunk of the tree will help to do this as the grass competes with the tree for nutrients and water. Conversely, if a tree in a lawn is not growing as strongly as you would like, strip off a circle of turf immediately around the tree. Mulching the bare soil with gravel will help prevent weed growth.

A mulch can also be applied around nearly all trees and shrubs in spring, to smother weed growth and conserve soil moisture. Make sure the soil is thoroughly moist before you apply the mulch, otherwise it may simply prevent rain penetrating the soil. Shredded bark, cocoa shell, garden compost and similar materials can be used for mulching, as with border plants.

While the main planting season for deciduous bare-root trees and shrubs is autumn and winter, evergreens do best when planted in mid- to late spring. If the weather is particularly warm or dry, make sure the roots have adequate moisture, but avoid making the soil too wet, since this could prevent roots establishing properly.

Deciduous trees and shrubs can also be planted now if they have been grown in containers. In theory, container-grown specimens can be planted all year round, but spring is often one of the best times, particularly in very cold areas, or when slightly tender subjects are being planted. Remember to water the plants regularly, as spring-planted specimens will be very prone to damage from drying out all through the summer following planting.

Evergreens like the common holly tree or bush are especially prone to high winds and drying conditions because of their year-round complement of foliage.

Avoid transplanting or disturbing sensitive evergreen trees such as the magnificent *Magnolia grandiflora*.

Garden FERTILIZERS

Plants need a whole range of chemical nutrients which, for the most part, they take up from the soil, where the chemicals occur naturally. However, where natural chemical nutrients are in short supply, they can be provided by the application of fertilizers.

IN CERTAIN conditions, there may not be enough chemical nutrients available in the soil – if there are a lot of plants tightly packed together, for example, or if the same type of plant has been grown in the same spot for several years, gradually depleting the soil of its nutrient supply. This is when fertilizers can be of assistance.

There are many different types of fertilizer available to gardeners, supplying different nutrients in different formulations. If the wrong type is applied, or at the wrong time, it may be completely wasted – or even worse, it could end up damaging the plants.

The major nutrients a plant needs are nitrogen, phosphorus and potassium, and these are those most likely to be in short supply and which need to be applied to the soil on a regular basis. There are lots of other essential chemicals too, such as calcium, iron, magnesium, manganese, molybdenum and boron; these are generally needed in only small amounts and are less likely to be deficient.

> **Plants need feeding more often if they are:**
> - vigorous growers
> - planted in soilless compost
> - growing in small containers
> - planted very closely
> - given short-acting fertilizers
>
> **Plants need feeding less often if they are:**
> - slow growing and compact
> - growing in good-quality loam-based compost
> - spaced well apart
> - have a good depth of soil for their roots
> - fed with slow-release, long-acting fertilizers

Fertilizers – both traditional organic and inorganic, now come in many different forms, in granules, liquid and powder. Slow-release fertilizers are particularly useful time savers: they are specially formulated to break down gradually, so releasing their nutrients steadily over a long period. This means that one application in spring is often sufficient to last for a whole season.

These lupins show vigorous, healthy growth – the result of careful fertilizing.

need to be in solution before the plants can absorb them. Organic fertilizers are obtained from animal or plant products, and tend to release their nutrients slowly, as they are gradually broken down and dissolve. Inorganic fertilizers are manufactured or mined; the nutrients they contain tend to be more concentrated, more soluble and so more quickly available to plants.

Spring is a useful time to apply fertilizers to the soil because the plants are growing strongly and actively taking up nutrients. There is little point in applying a soluble, fast-acting fertilizer to the soil in winter – it will be washed away by rain before the plants can use it. Perhaps the most important nutrient for spring use is nitrogen, required in large quantities by plants as they make rapid growth. Potassium is also particularly valuable for those plants that are forming their flower buds.

Fertilizers that can be applied in spring come in the form of granules, powder or liquid: liquid fertilizers have the fastest effect and give a quick boost to plants. They can be watered on to the soil around the plants, and some types can be sprayed directly on the foliage.

Powder and granules dissolve quite quickly in the soil moisture and are scattered over the soil around the plants. Further applications of fertilizer are generally required throughout the spring and summer months; check individual packs for detailed directions.

Particular care should be taken when fertilizing plants in containers. Take care to keep the fertilizers off the plants themselves since they can scorch stems and foliage; if the soil is dry, water fertilizers in soon after application.

Plants such as this pretty red sweet pea will nearly always benefit from fertilizers, producing brighter, healthier flowers. Remember, though, that too much fertilizer will do even more damage than a shortage.

Generally, nitrogen is needed for leafy growth, phosphorus for root growth and potassium for flower and fruit production (though this is a simplified summary of what are actually very complex roles in plant growth). Compound fertilizers contain varying proportions of the three nutrients, which are stated on the label.

Fertilizers are available in many different forms, but the nutrients always

Spring LAWN REPAIRS

A well-kept lawn really sets off the rest of the garden for most of the year, but unfortunately over the winter lawns do not look their best. However, as soon as spring arrives, the grass perks up. This is the time for gardeners to act, to make sure the lawn looks its best all through the summer months.

A well-tended lawn is a visual delight that will serve as the centrepiece of almost any garden.

Tidy edges with a sharp edging iron and cut to a plank for a straight edge or to a hose for curves. Trim off as little as possible.

LAWNS HAVE to put up with a great deal of wear and tear, but during the winter, the grass is least able to cope with it. Walking over the lawn in wet conditions compacts the soil, leading to poor growing conditions; walking on the grass in frosty weather crushes the frozen leaf blades and kills them. Patches of grass in heavily used spots may die out altogether, leaving ugly bald patches,

and lawn edges are easily damaged, breaking and crumbling away with careless treatment. Cold weather and low light levels mean that regenerative growth is very slow to take place.

Spring is the season to start putting all this right. The first job is to rake off any fallen leaves or other debris. Scatter or remove molehills and wormcasts if they are present, otherwise they will be flattened and spread by the mower, smothering patches of grass. Give the lawn a preliminary mowing, with the blades of the mower set high to just tip the grass.

Check lawn edges; they may only need trimming with long-handled

edging shears to neaten them up. If they are generally untidy and indistinct, however, they will probably need to be recut – neat edges are very important to the lawn's overall appearance (see opposite, bottom left).

If the edges are broken and damaged in just one or two places, this can be easily repaired. With an edging iron, cut out a rectangle of turf to include the damaged portion, making sure all the sides are straight. Lift the section of turf by undercutting it with a sharp spade, turn it 180° so that the damaged portion is now on the inside, and re-lay it in the same place, lining up the straight edge with the lawn edges. Fill in the damaged area with some good-quality garden soil and sow it with a little lawn seed. Make

sure the relaid turf does not dry out over the next few weeks, and the repair should soon be invisible.

Bare patches which have developed over the winter can also be dealt with now (see below). These usually occur because of heavy use, and it may be worth considering laying a solid path or stepping stones over a well-worn route to avoid damage to the grass in future. It is often difficult to match the colour and texture of the existing lawn with grass from seed, so if the bare patch is in a very conspicuous place, cut out a square of turf to include the bald patch and replace it with a turf lifted from a less conspicuous area of the lawn, where it can be reseeded without the differences being too obvious.

A non-grass lawn can make an attractive alternative to the conventional garden centrepiece, although it may require greater attention.

Thyme is a hardy and relatively durable ground cover plant with aromatic leaves. It makes an attractive and colourful lawn.

Chamomile has been used as an alternative lawn plant for centuries. It looks and smells marvellous, but requires attentive care.

Some of the hardier varieties of *Hedera* (ivy), with their extensive and very rapid growing habit, do well as ground cover plants.

REPAIRING BARE PATCHES IN LAWNS (1)
Fork over and then dig out the affected area, lifting out the top soil. Mix as much of the top soil as possible with grass seed and a small amount of sowing compost. Spread the mixture evenly all over the affected area with a hand trowel.

REPAIRING BARE PATCHES IN LAWNS (2)
Use a straight piece of timber to compact the mixture into the affected area and smooth it down until it is level with the surrounding lawn. Protect the newly sown area from birds by covering it with horticultural fleece or netting.

Mowing, Feeding, WEEDING

Once repairs have been made, it is time to cater for the rest of the lawn's needs.

THE MOST obvious task, which needs to be undertaken at frequent intervals for the rest of the spring and summer, is mowing.

Grass is a resilient plant which will continue to thrive despite having a

exceptions being high-quality, 'bowling green' lawns composed of fine-leaved grasses, which can be cut to half this height. Lawns that are mown too closely have less drought resistance, less vigour and more weeds, and do not have that lovely, rich green colour.

Grass on the spring lawn is likely to be quite long. The first cut should be very light, just removing the tips of the leaf blades. The mower height should gradually be lowered on subsequent cuts until the correct height is reached, but to avoid a check to growth, no more

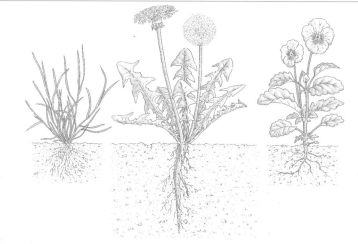

HOW PLANTS GROW

Lawns are usually made from grasses because their growth point is at the base of the stem, so they can be walked on and cut without it affecting their growth. Plants such as dandelions form a ground-hugging rosette, so mowing does not damage them and they can become lawn weeds. Other types of plant, which have their growing point at the tip of the shoot, will be killed by repeated mowing.

There is an art to good mowing, involving care with the height of the blades and careful changes of direction.

proportion of its leaves regularly removed – something few other plants would put up with. By cutting the grass we can transform it into a thick, springy turf, which is both attractive and functional. However, it is important not to cut the grass too close, otherwise the turf is weakened and the lawn loses both its vigour and its pleasing appearance. Most lawns should be cut no lower than 2.5cm (1in), the

FEEDING THE LAWN
Some fertilizers can be applied as solids – powder or granules. They are most easily laid with a calibrated fertilizer spreader, which will ensure even coverage as it is pushed up and down the lawn.

than one-third of the growth of the grass should ever be removed at one time.

For the best results, mow the lawn in opposite directions each time you cut it – first up and down and then from side to side. Make sure the blades of the mower are kept well sharpened and are correctly aligned to give a clean cut.

Feeding and weeding the lawn

Like all plants, grass needs a steady supply of nutrients. During the spring, nitrogen is the most important nutrient, to stimulate lush, green growth. Choose a lawn fertilizer that is specially formulated for spring and summer use – this will contain the high proportion of nitrogen required.

Fertilizers may be applied as either solids (see left) or liquids. Liquid fertilizers can be applied through a watering can or more easily through a hose-end dilutor: they give rapid results and reduce the risk of scorching.

Weeds afflict nearly all lawns at some time or another. Where there are just a few isolated weeds, these can be removed by digging them out by hand. If there are a lot of weeds, the normal method is overall treatment of the lawn with a selective chemical weedkiller, which will destroy lawn weeds without damaging the grass. Selective weedkillers are applied as dry granules through a fertilizer spreader or as liquids through a sprayer or watering can fitted with a dribble bar.

Most lawns contain weeds, usually broad-leaved plants, which spoil the velvet texture and even colour of the grass. Here are some common examples.

Taraxacum officinale (dandelion) is a universal invasive weed.

Plantago major (greater plantain) is a hardy perennial with resistance to mowing.

The rampaging *Agropyron repens* (couch grass) has a wide-spreading rhizome.

Dealing with GARDEN PESTS

It is important to identify insects correctly to avoid killing those that are beneficial, such as ladybirds.

The plants in every garden are vulnerable to attack by pests. Sometimes the damage they cause is hardly noticeable; sometimes it can be devastating.

ALTHOUGH PESTS may be present all through the year, spring is the time when they start to make their presence felt with a vengeance. A pest might be defined as a creature which, through its natural lifestyle, damages garden plants or prevents them reaching their full potential. These are some of the pests that you are most likely to come across in the spring garden.

There are many different species of beetle, some helpful, others, such as this vine weevil, disastrous.

Aphids suck the sap of plants and cause extensive damage very quickly.

Aphids Aphids are small, soft-bodied animals in a variety of colours according to species; both winged and non-winged types occur. They reproduce with great speed and ease; female aphids take as little as seven days to mature and give birth to live young without the need for fertilization or mating. Each aphid has the potential to produce many thousands of offspring.

Aphids feed by sucking sap from the plants, and are particularly numerous at the tips of young shoots and clustered around flower buds. Their feeding weakens the plant, and their sheer weight of numbers can cause severe distortion of plant growth. Aphids are also responsible for the spread of virus diseases between plants, and they excrete a sticky honeydew, which can result in the growth of a disfiguring and damaging fungus known as sooty mould.

Beetles Beetles are by no means always bad news in the garden – there are

Plants are particularly vulnerable to pests in

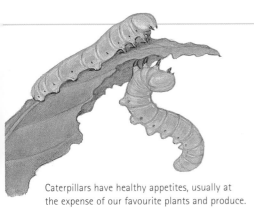

Caterpillars have healthy appetites, usually at the expense of our favourite plants and produce.

Red spider mites (shown here greatly enlarged), feed on the underside of plants' leaves and can cause serious damage, especially in the greenhouse.

several species that are valuable allies in the fight against pests, including ladybirds and ground beetles. However, there are quite a few which can cause a great deal of damage.

In late spring, the spectacular cockchafers are on the wing – huge, clumsy brown beetles making loud, droning flights on warm evenings. There are also several other, smaller varieties of chafer beetle. While the adults can cause damage to young leaves and flowers, particularly on roses and apples, it is the fat, C-shaped, dingy white, soil-living larvae that do most harm, fatally attacking the roots of many ornamental and kitchen garden plants.

Another beetle on the wing in mid- to late spring is the raspberry beetle, which lays its eggs in the flowers of raspberries, blackberries and hybrid

berries; larvae hatch to turn up as maggots in the fruit when it is harvested. Flea beetles – small, brown beetles which jump around the plants like fleas – eat small holes in the leaves of members of the cabbage family as the seedlings emerge from the soil; they may also attack various seedling bedding plants. Weevils, a distinctive type of long-snouted beetle, attack a very wide range of plants.

Caterpillars These are the larvae of various moths and butterflies. Like all larvae, their principal aim in life is to eat, and just a single caterpillar can destroy a huge amount of plant tissue. Cabbage caterpillars attack all types of brassicas in the kitchen garden; tortrix, codling and winter moths home in on fruit trees, while caterpillars of moths such as the angleshades and vapourer cause problems among ornamental plants.

Slugs and snails Mainly night-time feeders, slugs and snails particularly target the young growth of border plants and seedling vegetables, but they have wide-ranging feeding habits. They are often present in large numbers after dark, and can reduce leaves to a skeleton of veins overnight.

Leaf miners are the larvae of several different species of insect, including moths and sawflies. They tunnel into leaves, causing ugly, widespread disfigurement.

Scale insects are tiny, limpet-like creatures which cling to the stems of many plants, slowly sucking the sap out of them. They are both unattractive and dangerous, causing slow yet extensive damage.

Slugs and snails prefer warm, moist conditions and feed voraciously at night.

spring, when they produce tender new shoots

Controlling GARDEN PESTS

Pests will ruin both ornamental garden displays and kitchen garden crops if left to their own devices. The severity of pest attacks varies from year to year, but it is always necessary to keep an eye on the situation so that you can take action to prevent a problem getting out of hand.

Marigolds interplanted with vegetables deter carrot fly and brighten up the plot.

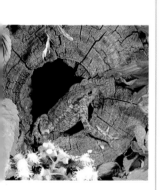

Toads and frogs are welcome in the garden, since they will keep plants free from slugs and other pests. Encourage them to visit by providing a pond in which they can lay their eggs and places where they can hibernate.

THERE ARE two main ways to approach the pest problem – by using chemical pesticides, or by using non-chemical, organic methods. Most gardeners use a combination of the two, dealing with the pests by organic methods first, and then using chemicals only when there is a particularly bad infestation that is difficult to overcome by other means. It is quite possible to get by without using chemical pesticides at all, particularly if you are willing to accept a few imperfections among your plants.

Everyone should take the following steps to help keep garden pests under control, starting in the early spring.

1 Look after your plants. Producing strong, healthy plants will not make them immune to pest attack, but it will make them more able to shrug off damage. Choose pest-resistant varieties, if available; grow plants in the right soil and at the right spacing, feeding and watering them as necessary.

2 Be observant. Take time to look at your plants regularly, and you will soon develop an 'eye' for spotting problems – plants that are just not looking healthy, or are showing some abnormality of growth. Check particularly the vulnerable parts of plants – young shoots, flower buds, the undersides of leaves.

Do something before a problem becomes serious; don't just hope it will go away – it never does!

3 Act swiftly. As soon as you spot a potential problem, do something about it, before it becomes serious.

4 Take simple measures first. If you find a couple of caterpillars on your cabbage plant, pick them off. If aphids are clustered on a young sideshoot, break the sideshoot off, or hose the aphids off with a jet of water. If you catch the infestation in its early stages, this may be all the action you need to take.

Chemical pesticides There may be times when you need to take stronger measures. Any garden shop will provide you with a vast number of products promising swift death to a wide range of pests, but there are several points to bear in mind before you use any garden chemical.

Safety All garden pesticides have been rigorously tested for their safety to humans before they are allowed to be sold, but remember that they are only safe when used as directed by the manufacturers. Many of them contain potent chemicals that could damage wildlife and the environment if misused.

Efficacy Pesticides are also tested for their efficacy before they can be sold, but not all pesticides kill all pests. It is important to choose the right product for the particular pest you want to destroy.

Persistence Many of the problems that arose from the early use of pesticides were due to their persistence – the product did not break down and become harmless, but continued to exist in a damaging form throughout the food chain for many years. Modern pesticides are far less persistent. As a rule you should always apply the least persistent product that is suitable for your needs.

Resistance Insects are good at building up resistance to poisons that are used against them, which can eventually render some pesticides almost completely ineffective. It helps to overcome resistance if you vary the type of chemicals you use on your pests.

Many insects are the gardener's friends, living on plant-eating species.

(1) Lacewing – eats aphids; (2) Centipede – with a flat orange body eats small slugs; (3) Devil's coach horse – eats soil insects; (4) Ladybird – and larva – eat aphids; (5) Ichneumon – eats aphids; lays eggs in bodies of caterpillars; (6) Hoverfly – larva eats aphids; (7) Ground beetle – adult and larva eat insects, grubs and slugs.

Cultivating VEGETABLES

Spring is a busy time in the vegetable garden, with lots of sowings to be made in the garden and plants to set outside from sowings made earlier indoors.

THE VEGETABLE plot should have been dug over in autumn and winter; once the soil starts to dry out in spring it can be broken down further to prepare for sowing. Free-draining soils can be cultivated earlier in the year than heavy clays. A good spell of dry, sunny, breezy weather in early spring helps bring the soil to the right condition.

Fork over the dug ground, if necessary, breaking down large clods by giving a sharp smack with the back of the fork. Then use a rake to break the soil down further to fine, even crumbs and to level the surface, raking off any large stones, weeds or plant debris in the process. Raking is an art that needs practice: use a light touch with the rake and try to avoid trampling the soil too much while you are working.

Once the soil surface is level, seeds can be sown. Most vegetables are sown in straight rows by drawing out a drill – a shallow trench – across the plot. There are various ways of doing this. The most common is to stretch a garden line (or piece of twine tied between two sticks) across the plot, making sure it is taut. Then, using the line as a guide, pull out the drill with the corner of a draw hoe. Another method is to use the handle of the rake or hoe, laying it on the soil and pushing it in lightly to leave a shallow depression.

Sow the seeds thinly along the drill, either sprinkling pinches from the palm of your hand, or tapping out a thin stream from the corner of the seed packet. Once the row is sown, draw soil back evenly with a rake to fill the drill, then tamp the soil down with the flat of the rake to firm it.

Some seeds are not sown right down the length of the row but are spaced, or 'station sown'. These are seeds that are large enough to handle, such as peas and beans, and they are sown at roughly their final spacings, with allowances being

Narrow paths divide up this vegetable plot, providing easy access to the beds and giving it form.

When all danger of frost has passed, it is safe

Intensive cultivation means that plenty of fresh vegetables can be produced in a small area.

made for some failures in germination. Parsnips and beetroot, for example, are usually sown at three seeds to each station; if more than one germinates, the weaker seedlings are removed at a later stage. With some large, station-sown seeds such as beans it is not even necessary to draw out a drill – simply push the seeds into the prepared soil.

Seedlings which have been sown under cover and fully hardened off can be planted out when they reach an appropriate size and once the weather conditions are right.

Handle the young plants by their leaves rather than their stems, knocking them out of their trays or pots and disentangling the roots as carefully as possible to avoid damage. Make a planting hole with a trowel or dibber (again using a garden line as a guide for straight rows) and set each plant in the planting hole so that its roots are in good contact with the soil. Firm plants in using your knuckles, the sole of your boot or the trowel, depending on the size and type of plant. The soil for planting should be prepared in much the same way as for sowing, but it is best to choose a cool, showery spell for the planting itself, since this helps the new plants establish quickly and prevents them wilting.

Once all danger of frost has passed, it is safe to plant out seedlings that have been sown under cover, such as runner beans and sweetcorn.

Knock the plant out of its pot, placing your hand over the surface of the compost with the main stem between your fingers.

Dig a planting hole with a hand trowel or dibber and carefully place the plant in the soil, again trying not to handle the stem or leaves.

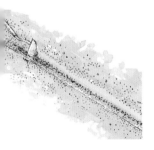

Ensure that the roots of the plant make good contact with the soil and then firm in the dug out soil around the base of the plant.

PLANTING SEEDS IN DRILLS
Mark out the line of planting you wish to achieve with a piece of twine or a hosepipe and then draw out a drill – or shallow trench – using a hoe. Place the seeds evenly along the length of the drill, remove the marking out line and then rake the displaced soil back over the row of seeds. Finally, tamp the soil down firmly with the back of the rake.

to set out plants that have been sown indoors

Kitchen Garden WEEDING

Spring is the time when all plants are starting into growth – and that includes weeds. Weeds can severely reduce the kitchen garden harvest, or even cause crops to fail altogether. They also look untidy and sometimes harbour damaging pests.

Hoeing will shave the tops off weeds, weakening or killing them, but a hoe should not be used to dig out roots.

the entire weed, preventing regrowth, and taking the weeds away makes the weeded area look neat and tidy. The most obvious disadvantage of this method is that it is time-consuming, and often back–breaking work.

IT OFTEN takes a concerted attack, using a combination of different methods, to keep weeds under control. A primary rule is to take action early: not only does this make weeds easier to eliminate, but it limits the damage they are able to do to crops. In certain situations it is possible to prevent a large amount of weed growth by using mulching materials efficiently.

The main weapons against existing weeds are:

Hand weeding This means pulling weeds out of the soil by hand, or with the help of a trowel or hand fork. Its advantages are that it should remove

Hoeing The hoe offers an excellent way of dealing with young, seedling weeds, especially in the vegetable garden where crops are grown in straight rows. The object of hoeing is to kill the young weeds by slicing them off at soil level. Hoe in bright, dry, preferably breezy weather to ensure that the decapitated weeds wilt and die quickly. Damp weather gives the weeds the opportunity to regrow. The advantages of hoeing are that it is relatively quick to undertake and can be carried out without bending over. The disadvantages are that weather conditions must be right for a good result and it is easy to damage crop plants with the hoe.

Flame gun This is a less common method of weed control but can be very effective. An intensely hot flame, powered by petrol or gas cylinders and usually guarded by a shield, is passed over the area of weeds, which quickly shrivel and die. Advantages of this method are that it is quick, not difficult to carry out, can be used in damp conditions where hoeing would be ineffective, and burns up weed debris. Disadvantages are that it is easy to damage cultivated plants through carelessness, and that it is only suitable for fairly large areas of vacant soil. A flame gun is potentially dangerous if misused, which makes some gardeners nervous about using one.

Chemical herbicides There are several different types of herbicide with varying methods of action for different

WEEDING WITH CHEMICAL HERBICIDES
Apply chemical herbicides with a dribble bar on a watering can, but make sure that the weedkiller does not fall on any other plants.

situations, crops and weeds. They vary from paraquat, a 'chemical hoe' which kills the topgrowth but has no effect on the soil or roots, to translocated weedkillers such as glyphosate which are carried around the whole plant from an application to one part of it. They are easy to apply through a sprayer or sometimes as granules, and translocated and soil-acting weedkillers prevent regrowth. On the debit side, they are not suitable for organic gardeners (as the other methods mentioned are) and they need suitable weather conditions. Herbicide-treated weeds also look unattractive when they die.

A plastic sheet mulch laid over bare ground will clear it of weeds by smothering them as they germinate and depriving them of light and water.

Convolvulus arvensis (field bindweed) is a common perennial with deep roots and a creeping habit which is very difficult to eradicate.

Ranunculus repens (creeping buttercup) is a perennial which spreads rapidly by runners and also by seed.

Senecio vulgaris (groundsel) is an annual with seeds that have threadlike appendages and are easily dispersed by the wind.

Fruit TREES AND BUSHES

Fruit-tree blossom is an attractive sight in spring. It is also a vital stage in the production of the entire fruit crop – there can be no fruit without it.

Apples trees bloom in mid-to late spring and the pink buds, opening to white, stamen-filled flowers, are irristible to pollinating insects.

TREES AND BUSHES are sometimes reluctant to produce a good show of blossom, and this may be due to lack of potassium. A high-potassium fertilizer such as sulphate of potash applied in early spring and again in autumn will encourage good flowering.

When fruit buds are just swelling in very early spring, birds can be a real problem. A number of birds, notably bullfinches, peck at the swelling buds and destroy them; they often work in flocks and can do a lot of damage. At this time of year, strips of glittery foil hung in the branches of trees, or similar bird-scaring devices, may help to keep birds away.

Even when plenty of blossom is present, it usually has to be pollinated in order to produce fruit. Fruit trees which flower in very early spring, such as peaches, apricots and nectarines, often need to be pollinated by hand, as there are few pollinating insects about at that time of year. Use a soft paintbrush to transfer pollen from one flower to another. These early-flowering plants may also need to be protected against frost, which will kill the blossom; use fleece, sacking or old, lightweight curtains draped over the trees on nights when frost is forecast.

Later-flowering fruit is normally pollinated efficiently by bees and other pollen- and nectar-gathering insects, but it is very important not to spray fruit with insecticides against pests during the flowering season – most insecticides are non-selective, and will kill pollinating insects as well as the pests. Not all fruit has to be pollinated, but most fruit is a better shape and size when it has been, even if pollination is not essential for its formation.

Disease watch Fruit of all kinds is subject to a number of diseases, and some gardeners like to carry out a fungicide spraying programme, starting in spring, to protect against disease attack. There are several suitable fungicides that will give fruit plants protection against disease, and they can be used as a preventive as well as a cure. Follow the pack directions when spraying and start early in the season.

Gooseberries come in a number of different varieties, but not all have very good resistance to diseases.

Raspberries, blackberries and hybrid berries are making plenty of growth now, and the canes should be tied in to their supports as they grow.

A well-kept orchard in full blossom is a wonderful sight and holds the promise of summer plenty.

Weed control Keep fruit trees, bushes and canes free from weeds (see pages 44–45). Herbicides such as simazine can be used up to the woody stems and trunks of bushes and trees without damage to the plants. Once weeds have been removed, fruit benefits from a mulch of well-rotted compost, which will keep down further weed growth and retain soil moisture.

Berry care In late spring, strawberries are surrounded by straw to prevent the developing fruits being spoiled by contact with the ground, but this mulch should not be applied too early. Bare soil radiates more heat than soil covered by straw, and this heat can prevent the strawberry flowers being killed by late frosts. Alternatively, try one of the new solar heat mulches instead of straw.

Strawberries are one of the most rewarding of the soft fruit crops, being attractive, tasty and relatively easy to cultivate and look after.

Water GARDENING

A water feature can transform any garden, offering opportunities for almost unparalleled variety and liveliness.

A pool or water feature is a great addition to a garden, attracting wildlife and providing a place to grow a whole new range of beautiful plants.

LATE SPRING is the time to take care of established pools, to ensure that they stay in brilliant condition.

Controlling algae Increasing sunlight and warmth frequently lead to an explosion of unwanted growth in the pond in spring – that of the tiny algae that occur naturally in the water.

Although the algae does not look attractive, it is not actually doing any harm to either fish or plants. Its growth can be reduced or prevented by cutting down the amount of light entering the pond by growing plants with floating leaves to shade the water; water hawthorn and water lilies are good choices. Sufficient oxygenators, such as *Elodea canadensis* (Canadian pondweed) should be planted in the bottom of the pool to use up nutrients in the water and supply it with oxygen to keep it healthy and clear.

As long as the right balance of plants and fish are present in the pool, cloudy water in spring should be a temporary occurrence for which no action need be taken. As the cultivated water plants increase their growth, they will take care of the algae on their own.

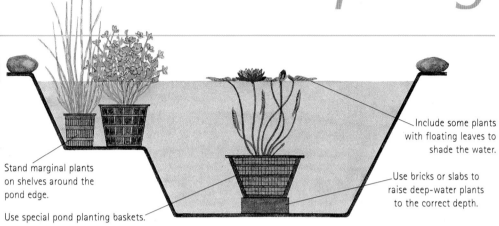

Include some plants with floating leaves to shade the water.

Stand marginal plants on shelves around the pond edge.

Use special pond planting baskets.

Use bricks or slabs to raise deep-water plants to the correct depth.

Aquatic and marginal plants are numerous and varied. Here are a few:

Ceratophyllum demersum (hornwort) grows vigorously and helps to oxygenate the water and provide a habitat for aquatic insects.

PLANTING A POND

Variety is the key to a successfully planted pond. Mix colours, textures, shapes and height as you would elsewhere in the garden, and use special pond planting baskets to prevent soil from escaping.

Thinning overgrown plants

Oxygenating plants often grow very rapidly and are sometimes in danger of overfilling the pond. Lilies and other deep-water aquatics, too, can outgrow their space. Late spring is a good time to reduce the growth of such plants by removing them from the water, splitting them up by hand or with a sharp knife, and replanting healthy portions back into the pool.

Feeding fish

Fish are important in ponds, not just to add colour, life and interest, but to eat the various insects that would otherwise breed in the water and cause a nuisance. Feeding fish in the spring and summer helps to keep them healthy and ensures they have plenty of reserves for overwintering. If they are fed regularly, they quickly become surprisingly tame, and will soon take food from the fingers if you have a little patience.

Making a new pond

If you don't have a pool in the garden, late spring is the best time of year to make one. Either use a preformed fibreglass shell, excavating a hole to fit, or dig a hole to the required dimensions and line it with a sheet of butyl rubber. Plant a range of oxygenating plants, deep-water aquatics with floating leaves, and some marginals on a shelf around the edge.

A waterfall or fountain is a useful addition to any pond, helping to keep the water fresh and clear as well as being attractive in its own right.

Nymphaea (water lilies) are perennial water plants grown for their floating, rounded leaves and beautifully coloured flowers.

The many different species of water lily can be used selectively to provide strong colour contrasts across any pool or pond.

Iris laevigata, a beardless Japanese iris, grows tall on the margins of ponds and in other very damp sites, standing out and providing shade.

Looking After WILDLIFE

It is relatively easy to plant your garden with the interests of wildlife in mind. Birds enjoy the seeds of sunflowers, butterflies are attracted to buddleja.

Garden wildlife means the wild animals, birds, insects and reptiles that visit or make their homes in our gardens.

THE TERM wildlife is generally taken to mean those species we find attractive or interesting, and not the ones we class as garden pests. However, there is a lot of overlap between 'wildlife' and pests, with some species playing dual roles. They may be valuable in one season and damaging in another: wasps, for instance, are a nuisance in late summer, when they eat ripe fruit and sting at the slightest provocation, but for most of the season they are helpful to gardeners, consuming large numbers of potential plant pests such as aphids. Other species may be exclusively damaging – squirrels stripping the bark from young

Spring is the time to think about providing food for animals later in the year

trees; deer eating the tops of trees and shrubs; badgers digging holes in lawns in search of soil-living grubs – but are so attractive and fascinating to many people that they are welcomed into the garden despite the damage they cause.

If you enjoy the sight of wildlife in the garden, there are many ways in which it can be encouraged, but you must be willing to accept the possibility of some damage to plants in return. In general, the effect of increased wildlife populations tends to be a positive one as far as gardeners are concerned.

Spring

A wildflower meadow is an ideal home for garden wildlife.

Winter is a lean time of year when natural food is scarce, and many species of bird can be attracted to the garden by the regular provision of food. In spring, however, natural food sources become plentiful, and it is time gradually to reduce the amount of food supplied, stopping altogether in the nesting season – the foods we provide are not necessarily healthy for baby birds and could be harmful. Water should continue to be supplied all the year round, however, including water for bathing as well as for drinking.

Nest boxes provided in very early spring can encourage various species

If you wish to attract wildlife into your garden, make sure that there is a constant supply of clean water.

of bird to raise their young in our gardens. Make sure the boxes are of the right design and proportions for the species you want to encourage; bird societies can supply detailed plans. If you have existing nest boxes in place, clean out any debris they may contain before the new nesting season begins. As well as nest boxes for birds, you could try putting up special boxes as summer roosting places for bats – many bats are endangered species and could do with all the help they can get.

Spring is the time to think about providing a natural food supply for birds and animals next autumn and winter, by sowing or planting species such as thistles and sunflowers for their seedheads, cotoneaster, holly and brambles for their fruits, and even cultivating a patch of stinging nettles to provide food for butterfly larvae. It is also time to plant scented flowers which will attract butterflies and moths later in the summer: *Sedum spectabile* (ice plant), buddleja, honeysuckle, petunia, sweet tobacco plant and night-scented stock among them.

A garden pond, even a small one, will be popular with a very wide variety of useful and interesting wildlife species. Frogspawn from other garden ponds (don't remove it from the wild) will help get frogs established if they don't find the pond by themselves, but frogs, toads and newts often turn up magically once a pond is installed.

Wildlife is good for gardens. Birds, insects and other animals all play their part in maintaining the balance of nature.

A nest box, tucked away among foliage, but out of the reach of predators, will quickly attract small garden birds such as this robin.

A valuable pollinator and consumer of aphids and their larvae, the hoverfly is often mistaken for a pest, but it can be recognized easily by its hovering flight.

Moths, both day- and night-flying species, are also useful pollinators in the garden and some, such as the large hawk moth, are as brightly coloured as butterflies.

Softwood CUTTINGS

Many plants can be readily propagated from cuttings taken from the new growth they have made in spring. The time the cuttings are taken depends on the type of plant and where it is growing.

PLANTS IN A warm greenhouse or conservatory are likely to have produced suitable shoots for cuttings in early spring. For plants outside in the garden it may be late spring or early summer before there is sufficient new growth for propagation.

Softwood cuttings are normally very easy to root. Little equipment is required; a clean seed tray or pot with a plastic propagator cover, a supply of sterile compost, a sharp knife or razor blade and a pencil or dibber are useful. For most gardeners, a half-size seed tray is often large enough, since this will hold 12–15 cuttings; a 9cm (3½in) pot will hold up to half a dozen, depending on the type of plant being propagated.

Clear plastic propagator covers are available to fit both pots and full and half-size trays. Covers for trays may have adjustable vents, which are very useful, allowing more control over the level of humidity around the cuttings. It is not essential to buy purpose-made propagator covers – you can improvise with clear plastic bags supported on split canes, or even empty plastic soft drinks bottles cut in half to cover a pot. Purpose-made covers do tend to be easier to use, though, and they are not expensive.

Compost used for rooting cuttings usually contains a low level of nutrients and a good proportion of sharp sand to ensure free drainage. The same compost is also suitable for seed sowing, and it is generally sold as 'seed and cuttings' compost (as opposed to potting compost) though increasingly, 'multi-purpose' composts, which can be used for both propagating and potting, are being produced. Composts may be based on soil (John Innes type), but soilless composts based on peat, or peat substitutes such as coir, are more popular for raising cuttings.

As the cuttings are prepared, they are cut to a suitable size and unnecessary leaves are removed from them. The base of the cutting is often trimmed to just below a node or leaf joint, since roots are generally produced more readily at this point. In some instances the cutting can simply be snapped from the plant and inserted straight into the compost, but where further trimming is necessary, a sharp blade must be used. If the blade is not sharp enough, the plant tissues will be crushed instead of being cut cleanly, and rotting, rather than rooting, will be the result. A single-edged razor blade,

Impatiens (busy lizzie) does well when propagated by the softwood cutting method in early spring.

Softwood cuttings are easy to root

Penstemon is a wide-ranging genus including many perennials and cultivars. It is a plant that lends itself well to propagation by softwood cuttings.

occurring naturally and to speed the rooting process. Many hormone rooting powders also contain a fungicide to prevent the cuttings rotting. While these products do have their uses, most softwood cuttings taken in spring do not need rooting powder – sometimes it can actually impede the rooting process. If it is used – for plants that are known to be slow or difficult to root, for example – only a very light dusting on the base of the stem should be given, or damage could be caused.

A dibber is used to make a hole in the compost to receive the cutting, and to firm it in after insertion; its tapering shape helps to ensure the base of the cutting is in firm contact with the compost. If you do not own a dibber, a pencil makes a handy substitute for the real thing.

Cuttings are taken from different plants at different times of the year. *Pelargonium* cuttings are taken in early spring from overwintered plants.

Chrysanthemum and *Argyranthemum* cuttings should be taken in spring, also from overwintered plants.

or more safely, a razor blade fitted into a plastic cover, is often a better option than a knife.

Root production is stimulated by plant hormones which concentrate in the stem, and hormone rooting powder is sometimes used to supplement those

Propagate *Iberis sempervirens* by cuttings in midsummer.

and little equipment is required

Taking CUTTINGS

Softwood cuttings tend to wilt rapidly once cut from the parent plant, and have no roots to take up water.

THE ATMOSPHERE around softwood cuttings must be kept humid in order to limit water loss from the cuttings while they are rooting.

1 Early morning is usually the best time to take cuttings, when plants are still

Delphiniums can be easily propagated by basal softwood cuttings in mid-spring.

fresh. The plants which are to be used to supply the cuttings should be watered well the night before to ensure the stems and leaves are not limp. Have everything you need ready before you remove the cuttings so that they can be prepared and inserted immediately. Select strong, healthy, typical shoots to use as propagating material, preferably without flower buds. Snap the selected shoot from the plant, or cut it with a knife or secateurs. When removing the cuttings material, cut the stems just above a leaf node, so that there is no stump left on the parent plant to rot back.

2 Reduce the cuttings to a suitable size, trimming with a razor-sharp blade to just below a leaf node. Most softwood cuttings should be around 7.5cm (3in) long when prepared, though this will vary according to the type of plant. Remove the lower leaves so that the cutting has two or perhaps three fully expanded leaves remaining. Sometimes the lower leaves can be pulled off easily, but pulling them away may damage the stem. It is better to remove them as closely as possible with a sharp blade. Try to remove all the leaf stalk cleanly, since any sections left may rot when they are below soil level.

3 Prepare trays or pots in advance, filling them with suitable compost then firming and levelling it with a presser – a piece of wood does the job very well.

Make a hole for the prepared cutting with your finger or a dibber and place the cutting in the hole, making sure that the base of the cutting is in contact with the compost. Firm the cutting into place gently, using your fingers. Continue until the tray is full, spacing the cuttings evenly so that the leaves do not touch.

4 Once the tray is full, water the compost and cuttings with a watering can fitted with a fine rose. Place the propagator cover on top, closing the vents if they are fitted. The cuttings should be left in a warm place, out of direct sun; it is a good idea to drape a piece of newspaper over the cover to start with, to supply some light shade. Softwood cuttings often wilt immediately after insertion, but they should pick up again in a few hours provided they are kept humid and shaded.

5 Check the tray daily to make sure the compost is still moist. In spring, cuttings often form roots very quickly, and some subjects may have started to root in 10 days or so; others may take much longer. It is usually quite easy to see when the cuttings have made good root growth because their centres start to look fresh and green and begin to grow away. Once they have reached this stage, they can be carefully turned out of the tray and potted up individually in fresh compost.

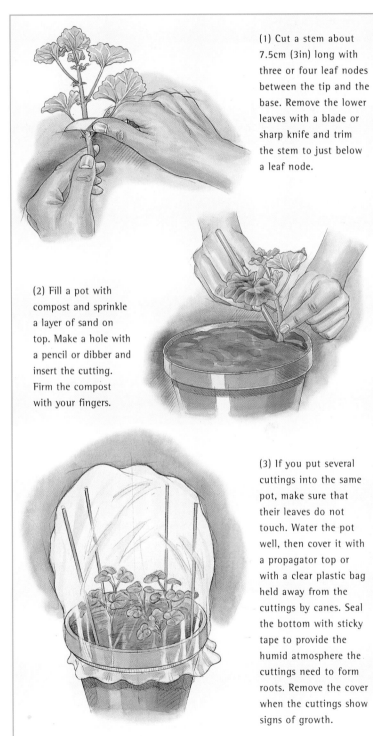

(1) Cut a stem about 7.5cm (3in) long with three or four leaf nodes between the tip and the base. Remove the lower leaves with a blade or sharp knife and trim the stem to just below a leaf node.

(2) Fill a pot with compost and sprinkle a layer of sand on top. Make a hole with a pencil or dibber and insert the cutting. Firm the compost with your fingers.

(3) If you put several cuttings into the same pot, make sure that their leaves do not touch. Water the pot well, then cover it with a propagator top or with a clear plastic bag held away from the cuttings by canes. Seal the bottom with sticky tape to provide the humid atmosphere the cuttings need to form roots. Remove the cover when the cuttings show signs of growth.

Plants for SPRING (1)

There is a host of plants, flowers, trees and bushes which express the unfolding beauty of this season. In spring everything comes alive after lying dormant during the autumn and winter months, and the annual challenge for the gardener is renewed.

A classic spring garden in full, vigorous bloom. The contrasting colours of these plants work particularly well.

IN THE EARLIEST days of spring, every new flower that comes into bloom is eagerly welcomed, but with each day that goes by more and more plants come into their own in a glorious rush of colour and fresh new growth. It is not only flowers that provide interest in the garden, but the new leaves that are unfolding – particularly finely shaped leaves of plants such as acers and the cut-leaved elder, *Sambucus racemosa* 'Plumosa Aurea'.

Heaths and heathers have been providing colour through the winter, and many continue into the spring. The many hybrids of *Erica carnea* are a good example; this heather is particularly useful because it will grow on slightly chalky soils as well as acid ones. *Calluna* is more fussy about soil, but it is worth providing a lime-free patch for cultivars such as 'Spring Cream' and 'Spring Torch', which have strikingly coloured new shoots at this time of year.

Catkins on hazel and willow are among the earliest signs of spring, as are some of the smaller varieties of

Spring

In early spring every new flower that comes into bloom is eagerly welcomed

narcissus, such as 'February Gold' and 'Tête à Tête'. Tulips come into their own in mid- and late spring, but again the smaller-growing varieties are earlier –

T. kaufmanniana and *T. griegii* have some fine early hybrids. Spring is the season of bulbs, and there are many to be enjoyed over the next few weeks, from the earliest *Anemone blanda* to the stately *Fritillaria imperialis* (crown imperial), as we head towards summer.

As the days lengthen and become warmer, so does the rate at which new flowering and foliage plants join the throng in our gardens. By late spring, there are many trees clothed in fresh green foliage, some of them producing spectacular and unusual flowers. *Cercis siliquastrum* (Judas tree) and *Paulownia tomentosum* (foxglove tree) are two that produce their blooms on bare branches before the leaves appear; *Davidia involucrata* (pocket handkerchief tree) waits until later to unfold its showy, white bracts. All three rarely fail to produce admiring comments.

Perennial borders start to burst into life in mid-spring, though their main season of interest is not until summer, but spring bedding makes sure that there is still plenty of bright colour to be enjoyed.

Salix helvetica is a spreading dwarf shrub with twiggy growth which sports woolly grey catkins in spring.

Fritillaria meleagris (snake's head fritillary) has bell-shaped flowers with chequered petals that begin to appear in late spring.

Crataegus monogyna (hawthorn) gives a beautiful display of blossom in spring and acts as a good, thorny windbreak or hedge.

Davidia involucrata (pocket handkerchief tree) is an unusual spring-flowering shrub with dramatic white bracts and black berries.

Plants for SPRING (2)

Spring-flowering plants are the very essence of a successful garden – the colour and form providers that every gardener identifies with most closely.

IF YOU ARE keen to create variety in your garden, there is no easier or better way to do it than by planting a vibrant mix of different spring-flowering plants. Here are some of the best and more widely available, for the entire season.

Early spring

Shrubs and trees

Acer rubrum
Calluna 'Spring Cream' and others
Camellia japonica
Chaenomeles speciosa,
  C. japonica
Chimonanthus praecox
Clematis armandii
Cornus mas

Primula vulgaris, the common primrose of meadows and woodlands, will thrive in the garden in moist soil in sun or light shade.

Corylopsis pauciflora
Corylus avellana 'Contorta'
Daphne odora 'Marginata',
  D. mezereum
Erica carnea varieties
Forsythia intermedia,
  F. suspensa
Hamamelis mollis
Magnolia stellata
Mahonia aquifolium
Prunus pissardii
Salix caprea
Viburnum tinus,
  V. burkwoodii
  V. bodnantense

Perennials and bedding plants

Aubrieta
Bergenia cordifolia
Doronicum
Primula vulgaris and others
Pulmonaria

Bulbs

Anemone
Chionodoxa
Crocus
Cyclamen coum
Eranthis
Erythronium
Hyacinth
Iris danfordiae,
  I. reticulata
Leucojum vernum
Muscari
Narcissus
Tulipa kaufmanniana and others

Daisy-like *Doronicum* (leopard's bane) is an early-blooming hardy perennial.

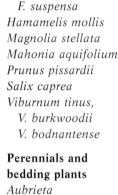

The many varieties of tulip are among the most colourful spring bulbs.

Mid spring

Trees and shrubs

Acer japonicum,
  A. palmatum
Amelanchier lamarckii
Berberis darwinii,
  B. stenophylla
Ceanothus
Clematis alpina,
  C. armandii
Cytisus praecox
Daphne burkwoodii,
  D. cneorum
Forsythia
Kerria japonica
Magnolia soulangeana,
  M. stellata

Malus
Osmanthus burkwoodii,
  O. delavayii
Pieris
Prunus in variety
Rhododendron
Ribes sanguineum
Rosmarinus officinalis
Skimmia japonica
Spiraea arguta
Ulex europaeus
Vinca major,
  V. minor

Perennials and bedding plants

Aurinia saxatilis
  (*Alyssum saxatile*)
Aubrieta
Bellis perennis
Bergenia
Cheiranthus cheiri
Doronicum
Epimedium

Bergenia cordifolia produces pink-purple bell-shaped flowers in early spring.

Euphorbia characias,
  E. polychroma,
  E. robbiae
Helleborus orientalis

Spring

Handsome Alliums, with umbels of pinkish lilac flowers, are hardy and easy to grow.

Hardy, evergreen *Ceanothus* 'Blue Cushion' is a compact bush covered in spring flowers.

Viburnum opulus,
*   V. plicatum*
Weigela
Wisteria

Perennials and bedding plants
Ajuga reptans
Aurinia saxatilis
*   (Alyssum saxatile)*
Aquilegia
Armeria
Aubrieta
Bergenia
Dicentra spectabilis
Euphorbia in variety
Geranium in variety
Geum
Helianthemum
Iberis
Incarvillea delavayii
Lithospermum
*   diffusum*
Nepeta mussini
Primula in variety
Saponaria
*   ocymoides*
Saxifraga umbrosa

Bulbs
Allium in variety
Anemone in variety
Convallaria majalis
Endymion non-
*   scriptus*
Fritillaria imperialis
Hyacinthus in
*   variety*
Leucojum aestivum
Narcissus in variety
Ornithogalum
Tulipa in variety

Forsythia x *intermedia* 'Lynwood' is a deciduous species with yellow flowers that wreathe its bare branches with a showy display in early spring.

The cup-shaped, pendulous blue flowers of *Clematis alpina* appear in late spring and are followed by silky seed heads.

Weigela florida 'Variegata' is a decorative, medium-sized shrub that flowers in late spring and looks well in most gardens.

Iberis sempervirens
Myosotis
Primula

Bulbs
Anemone
Chionodoxa
Convallaria majalis
Crocus
Erythronium
*   revolutum*
Fritillaria
*   imperialis,*
*   F. meleagris*
Leucojum vernum
Muscari
Narcissus
Tulipa fosteriana,
*   T. greigii,*
*   T. kaufmanniana*
*   and hybrids*

Late spring

Trees and shrubs
Aesculus
*   hippocastanum*
Berberis in variety
Buddleja globosa
Camellia japonica
Ceanothus
Cercis siliquastrum
Choisya ternata

Clematis montana
*   and large-flowered*
*   hybrids*
Crataegus
Crinodendron
*   hookerianum*

Cercis siliquastrum (Judas tree) bears purplish flowers in late spring.

The blue and white petals of early-flowering *Crocus chrysanthus* 'Blue Pearl'.

Cytisus
Daphne
Davidia involucrata
Deutzia gracilis,
*   D. rosea*
Elaeagnus
*   commutata*
Genista hispanica
Kerria japonica
Kolkwitzia amabilis
Laburnum
Magnolia
*   soulangeana*
Malus in variety
Mespilus germanica
Osmanthus
Paeonia
Pieris
Potentilla fruticosa
Prunus in variety
Rhododendron and
*   azalea*
Robinia hispida,
*   R. margaretta*
Rosmarinus
*   officinalis*
Sambucus racemosa
*   plumosa* 'Aurea'
Sorbus aria,
*   S. aucuparia*
Spiraea arguta
Syringa

Clockwise from top left: *Dahlia*
'Dark Stranger'; *Phlox paniculata*;
midsummer walled garden;
Hemerocallis 'Cynthia Mary';
sunflower; garden pond
in high summer.

Summer

HANGING BASKETS
Hanging baskets are especially prone to water loss. This is because they generally contain several different plants, all competing for the available water from a limited amount of soil. For this reason, baskets require very frequent watering.

roots; it also evaporates from the soil surface, especially in dry, sunny, or windy weather.

The water-holding capacity of the soil can be increased by digging in organic matter such as garden compost or manure in autumn or spring; these materials act like sponges to soak up water and hold it within range of the plants' roots. Easier to use at this time

of year, especially in containers, are water-retaining granules – sugar-like grains which absorb water to many times their own volume, forming a gel in the soil.

Once the earth around plants is thoroughly moist, the water can be kept in the soil by mulching, which prevents loss due to evaporation. Organic materials such as crushed cocoa shell and shredded bark are useful for mulching, as are inorganic materials such as pebbles and gravel. Apply any mulch thickly over the soil surface.

Water is often wasted by watering at the wrong time. Applying water in a fine spray in full sunshine means that a larger proportion of it is lost by evaporation; better to apply it early in the morning or in the cool of evening when it has more chance to penetrate the soil. The stage of growth of the plants is also important. For some vegetables and fruit, particularly, there are certain periods when water is valuable for increasing the yield: at other times, the water will be wasted in making a lot of leafy growth.

Apart from conserving water, which may be in short supply, taking sensible measures to avoid wasting water will also be of direct benefit to us all.

Some plants cope surprisingly well with a lack of water and drought conditions. Here are a few common examples.

Lavandula spp. (lavender), will happily tolerate dry, sunny conditions and often features in Mediterranean gardens as a result.

Cistus purpureus (rock rose) is another shrub with good resistance to a lack of water and bright sunlight. It is particularly good for coastal areas, since it also withstands salty sea winds.

Rosmarinus officinalis (rosemary) is a drought-resistant shrub grown for its aromatic leaves and used as a culinary herb.

which reduces evaporation loss

Watering METHODS

There are various methods of watering, some of them more efficient and easier to carry out than others. Which are most suitable depends on several factors, including the type of plants being watered.

This colourful, vibrant bed full of mixed *Salvia* 'Seascape' clearly demonstrates the benefits of carefully monitored watering. The plants are in prime condition, obviously receiving the moisture they require.

Watering can Straightforward and cheap, but hard work and not very efficient. Use a rose on the end of the spout to break up the water into a shower of droplets.

Hose Easier to use than a watering can, and capable of applying much greater volumes of water – something to be careful of when water conservation is a factor. A large number of different attachments is available.

Sprinkler This is fitted on the end of the hose and delivers water to a fixed area in a variety of spray patterns. It is useful because it can be left unattended, but may require a licence or be illegal to use in certain areas and situations.

Seep hose This is really a type of sprinkler, but instead of delivering water upwards into the air, water trickles out slowly along a length of perforated hose lying on the soil

GARDEN WATERING EQUIPMENT
Many different types of watering equipment are now widely available. (1) Garden hose on a reel. (2) Spiked bed sprinkler. (3) Revolving sprinkler. (4) Watering can fitted with a rose. (5) Arc lawn sprinkler.

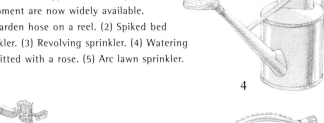

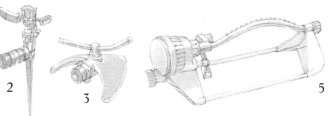

1

2

3

4

5

Sprinkler systems are versatile, with the facility to operate on an automatic timer and offering various spray patterns and degrees of watering.

surface. It gives better penetration than a sprinkler and is generally a more efficient method of watering.

Automatic watering systems These can be controlled by timers and they deliver water automatically for prearranged periods.

Trees and shrubs A length of pipe buried at the side of a tree or shrub at planting time will help to ensure water given through it penetrates deep into the soil, where the roots are. Several gallons should be given at a time if watering is necessary.

Containers require frequent watering. Use water-retaining granules in the compost and keep them out of drying winds.

Bedding plants Always water bedding plants thoroughly immediately before and after transplanting.

Lawns Avoid problems by not cutting the grass too short – never cut lower than 2cm (¾in), increasing the height to 4cm (1½in) during a drought. Water through a sprinkler when the grass starts to look dull, but before it turns yellow. Leave cuttings on the lawn to reduce moisture loss.

Vegetables and fruit Leafy vegetables such as cabbage need regular watering during dry spells; fruiting vegetables such as peas and beans need water most when they are flowering, to improve pod set.

An efficient method of watering plants in rows is the seep hose: perforated piping that leaks water throughout its length. Slow delivery means better penetration to the plants' roots.

Drip-feed irrigation systems work in much the same way as the seep hose, but are easier to monitor and use less water. The frequency of drip can be controlled by turning the individual taps positioned along the system's pipe.

Patio GARDENING

A patio is one of the most frequently used parts of the garden. Not only is it somewhere to sit and relax, but it is an excellent place to show off special plants, especially those in containers.

PATIOS ARE usually warm and sheltered, making them ideal places to grow some of the more tender and exotic specimens that might struggle to survive elsewhere.

Summer is the season when the patio comes into its own, and early summer is the time to check that everything is in good order.

Cleaning up Give the patio area a good sweep with a stiff brush, getting rid of the debris that has accumulated over the winter and spring, especially in the corners of walls. Dead leaves and plant remains make good hiding places for slugs and other garden pests as well as looking unsightly.

Safe paving Many patios are constructed from paving slabs and, over time, these can deteriorate. Slabs may be cracked or broken; settlement or poor laying can result in an uneven surface with protruding edges, which can be a serious hazard. Carry out any necessary repairs on a regular basis and throughout the year, re-laying or replacing slabs as necessary.

Lobelia is an excellent plant for low-level patio walls or to include in patio containers, since it will cascade freely, lighting up its immediate surroundings.

Care of decking
Wooden decking has become a popular material for patios, but it needs regular maintenance if it is to have a long life, especially in cool, damp climates. In early summer, check the timber carefully for damage, splitting or rot, replacing lengths if necessary. Clean the deck with a stiff brush and re-treat with a water-repellent wood preservative – choose a warm, dry spell for this. Check underneath the decking if possible to see whether weed growth at ground level needs to be controlled.

Timber sometimes becomes slippery in damp weather, and if this is a continuing problem, chickenwire can be tacked over the entire surface to provide a better grip. The wire will also need to be checked regularly to ensure that it has not become loose or rusted through, when it might present an additional hazard. Grooved timber used for decks is less likely to become slippery than smooth wood.

Dealing with damp Areas of the patio that are in permanent shade, or overhung by trees or roofs, may develop growths of moss or algae, especially over the winter months. This can make them dangerously slippery. There are

various proprietary cleaning products which will get rid of algae and moss in time for the main summer season.

Working on weeds
The cracks between paving slabs are often invaded by weeds, which will grow in tiny amounts of soil or debris. If the weed's roots spread beneath the slabs they are often difficult to pull out. A specially shaped patio weeding tool will help to hook out weeds, or they can be sprayed with path weedkiller and removed once the tops have died.

Overhanging plants Plants which spill over the edge of the patio help to soften

WEEDING BETWEEN PAVING SLABS
Use a specially shaped patio weeding tool to hook out weeds that are awkward to remove by hand. Ensure that you extract all the weeds' roots.

the hard lines of stone and brickwork, but after a few seasons they can get out of hand. Clip them back in early summer or when they have finished flowering. Lift up all overhanging plants and sweep away the debris that gathers beneath them.

Removing stains Spilt soil or compost, plant debris, grease from barbecues and spilt oil from garden machinery can all leave unsightly stains on paving which can be hard to remove. Diluted household bleach sometimes works, or there are proprietary stain removers that may give a better result.

Eccremocarpus scaber (glory vine) is a half-hardy, tendril climber that is good for training up over patio trellisses or other plants. It has light, graceful growth.

Clematis 'Perle d'Azur' is a vigorous, large-flowered climber that is often used to decorate the walls adjacent to patios. It flowers throughout the summer and is a real visual treat.

PATIO REPAIRS
Loose and cracked paving slabs should be replaced as soon as they become a problem. Use a cold chisel or crowbar to lift the slab and chip away any old mortar stuck to its underside. Lay a mixture of dry sand and cement in the hole left by the slab and rake and tamp it smooth. Replace the slab, bedding it down firmly and ensuring that it sits evenly. Finish off by brushing mixed dry sand and cement into all surrounding joints.

Rosa 'Aloha' has slow and limited growth, so it suits a restricted site such as a patio very well. It is a superb, fragrant rose that can easily be trained up surrounding walls and trellis.

Patio FRUIT & VEGETABLES

You don't need a large garden with a specially dedicated plot in which to grow fruit and vegetables – there are plenty of crops that can be grown in the minimum of space – and with very little work – on the patio.

CROPS CAN be grown in pots, tubs, raised beds and growing bags. If you intend to grow only a few vegetable plants, it is often not worth growing them from seed – most large garden centres, and many mail order seed merchants, will supply young plants in early summer.

Beans Both runner and french beans can be planted out in early summer, once the risk of frost is over. French beans can be grown in pots or growing bags; runner beans are best in deep tubs. Grow runner and climbing french beans up a wigwam of poles for support.

There are plenty of crops that grow in a minimum of patio space

Beetroot Baby beet varieties can be sown in a pot or growing bag. Space seeds about 2.5cm (1in) apart, and pull the roots once they are almost the size of a golf ball. Sow through to midsummer.

Carrots Choose stump-rooted or globe-shaped carrots and sow thinly in growing bags or tubs. Sow through to midsummer.

Courgette Set plants out in growing bags or pots in early summer, after the

Compact forms of apple trees do well in containers and will produce fruit in 2–4 years.

risk of frost has passed. Choose bush varieties. Water freely when flowering and when the fruits are swelling. Cut fruits regularly for continued cropping.

There is something particularly satisfying about growing your own produce, such as these apples, on the patio.

PLANTING UP A GROWING BAG
You will need a growing bag, a trough, plants, canes and string. Place the growing bag in the trough and cut out evenly spaced crosses in the top

Lettuce Mini lettuce such as 'Little Gem', 'Tom Thumb' and 'Blush' are good for growing bags or pots on the patio; 'cut-and-come-again' loose leaf varieties like 'Salad Bowl' are also useful. Sow until midsummer, thinning the seedlings out while small.

Peppers Suitable for sunny, sheltered positions, there are several compact varieties which are excellent for pots or growing bags. Set plants out in early summer, after the risk of frost.

Radish Very easy to sow direct in pots or growing bags and excellent for summer salads. Sow right through the summer for succession.

Tomatoes Buy plants and set them out in early summer, after the risk of frost. Select a compact outdoor bush variety; some, like 'Tumbler', are bred specially for patio growing. Water regularly and give high-potash liquid feeds.

Summer fruit on the patio

Strawberries are ideal patio plants; make sure they do not go short of water as the fruits form and are swelling. The developing fruits may need protection from slugs through the early summer months, but those grown in containers are usually less likely to be attacked.

Apples – especially the slender-stemmed 'Ballerina' and 'Maypole' trees – are suitable for patio growing in large tubs. Keep plants watered in dry spells. Pick the fruit when it parts easily from the spur; some varieties start cropping in mid- or late summer, while others are not ready for harvest until early autumn.

Blueberries grow well in large tubs of ericaceous (lime-free) compost, and their sweet, blue-black berries will need to be protected from birds as soon as they start to turn colour. The same goes for cherries; they make good trained trees against a patio wall or fence, growing in a raised bed.

Blueberries are an excellent summer soft fruit. They are very easy to grow but do require careful protection from birds.

Redcurrants are an early soft fruit that work well on patios since they are bushy, manageable plants.

side of the bag. Tuck the flaps under to form planting holes. Water the compost in the growing bag until it is thoroughly moist but not waterlogged. Use a trowel to dig planting holes

large enough to take your plants. Set the plants in the holes and provide suitable supports where necessary. As the plants grow, gently tie in the stems. Plant low-growing herbs to cover the bag.

Blackberries generally grow wild, but the thornless varieties can be cultivated in containers on the patio.

Summer GREENHOUSE CARE

The extra warmth and weather protection provided by a greenhouse or conservatory is very welcome in the cool days of spring, but during the summer keeping the temperature down can be a real problem. The sun on the glass soon sends temperatures soaring, and plants can be killed by heat and lack of water in a few hours.

A GREENHOUSE or conservatory should be a place to be enjoyed by both plants and people, but in unrelieved summer heat it can be a very uncomfortable place.

Ventilation Efficient ventilation is essential to allow hot air to escape and cooler air from outside to replace it, and keep the 'buoyant' atmosphere that both plants and people require. As well as vents in the roof, there should be at least one (depending on the size of the structure) lower level vent in the side

GREENHOUSE CARE IN THE SUMMER
Greenhouses and conservatories require constant attention during the summer months and should not be left untended for long periods unless they feature automated ventilation, watering, heating and humidity controls.

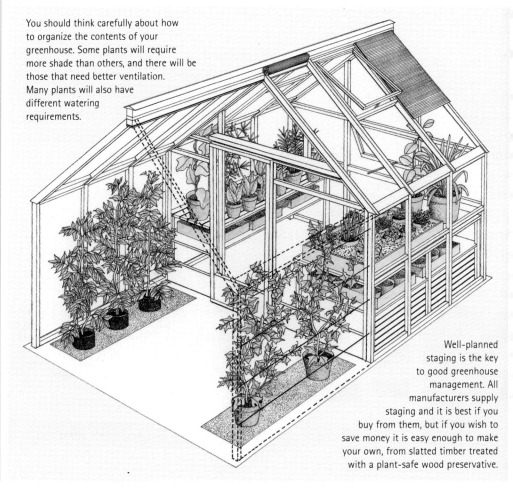

You should think carefully about how to organize the contents of your greenhouse. Some plants will require more shade than others, and there will be those that need better ventilation. Many plants will also have different watering requirements.

Well-planned staging is the key to good greenhouse management. All manufacturers supply staging and it is best if you buy from them, but if you wish to save money it is easy enough to make your own, from slatted timber treated with a plant-safe wood preservative.

Efficient ventilation is essential to allow hot air

In a climate where there is plenty of rain, alpine plants will do better in a greenhouse than in the garden, since they can be given the cool well-drained conditions they enjoy. If the pots are buried in coarse grit 10–15cm (4–6in) deep, the roots will remain frost free in winter and cool in summer.

A greenhouse environment offers the opportunity to grow more exotic plants from hotter climates. Here are a few of the best.

Iresine herbstii (beefsteak plant) is a bushy perennial which needs a good, loamy, well-drained soil and plenty of light to retain its brilliant purple-red leaf colour.

Pavonia x *gledhillii* grows best in hot-house conditions, requiring full light or partial shade and humus-rich, well-drained soil. Whitefly and red spider mite may be troublesome.

Variegated plants offer dramatic textures and colours and contrast well with other greenhouse and indoor plants.

walls. Extra vents should, if possible, be ordered when the greenhouse or conservatory is bought, but they can be fitted at a later date if necessary.

Automatic ventilators overcome the problem of windows needing to be opened on hot summer mornings before people are up and about. They are usually operated by a wax cylinder, which expands to open the vent as the temperature rises.

Shading Keeping direct sun out of the greenhouse or conservatory will play a great part in helping to reduce the temperature and avoid plant scorch. In most instances shading is applied to only a part of the structure, since

Greenhouses can sometimes be rather intrusive in the overall garden scene, but blend in well if painted green.

some plants prefer direct sun and bright conditions.

Paint-on shading material is cheap and easy to apply. It is usually mixed with water and applied to the outside of the glass with a brush or sprayer.

Blinds can be fitted to the outside or the inside of the greenhouse or conservatory. Their advantages are that they look neat, and can be rolled up out of the way on dull days.

Damping down In hot summer weather, splash water over the floor and staging of the greenhouse to cool the atmosphere and increase the humidity for the plants. Damping down should be carried out in the morning and early afternoon rather than in the evening.

to escape and cooler air to replace it

Pruning SHRUBS

Many spring- and early summer-flowering shrubs can be pruned as soon as flowering has finished if they are becoming untidy.

IT IS NOT essential to prune such shrubs every year, but it does help to prevent them becoming ungainly, and promotes strong new shoots to ensure plenty of flowers the following year.

When pruning flowering shrubs, it is important to know how the flowers are produced. Shrubs which flower in midsummer or later carry their flowers on new shoots that have been produced

following season. It is a good idea to remove some of the older, worn-out wood each year to encourage new growth.

Some basic rules of pruning apply, regardless of the type of plants being pruned (see opposite page).

A large shrub that does well in sunny, dry conditions, *Buddleja alternifolia* produces sweetly scented flowers on the drooping branches of the previous year's growth. Thin out the crown after flowering.

earlier in the year; they are pruned in winter or early spring to promote the maximum amount of new growth. Spring- and early summer-flowering shrubs, however, bear their flowers on branches that were produced the year before. Pruning immediately after flowering is over encourages the production of strong new growth that will carry flowers the

Reverted shoots

Varieties of shrubs that have variegated or coloured leaves sometimes produce plain shoots, which have reverted to the non-coloured growth of the parent species. These shoots should be cut out as soon as they are noticed; not only do they spoil the appearance of the selected variety, but they are normally stronger growing than the coloured shoots and, if left, will take over the entire shrub. Cut them right back to the main stem.

The same applies to varieties of shrubs with other features of interest, such as the corkscrew hazel (*Corylus avellana* 'Contorta'). This often produces straight stems among the more attractive twisted and contorted branches, and these non-typical shoots should also be cut out as soon as they are seen. This type of pruning can be carried out at any time of year – the unwanted shoots should not be allowed to develop for any longer than necessary.

Once the flowered branches have been removed, a proportion of the main stems should also be cut out – usually between a quarter and a third of the shrub, but this will vary from plant to plant. Stand back from the shrub and look at it carefully before making any cuts; choose the oldest, weakest and most awkwardly placed stems to be removed. The stems which are to remain should form a nicely balanced shape. Cut the selected stems right out, as near to the ground as possible; a pruning saw is often necessary as the branches may be quite tough. Reassess the shape of the plant as you remove each branch to maintain an attractive overall appearance.

Shrubs that benefit from pruning at this time of year include:

Buddleja alternifolia (butterfly bush)
Chaenomeles speciosa (japonica, Japanese quince)
Cytisus in variety (broom)
Deutzia gracilis (deutzia)
Forsythia intermedia (forsythia)
Kerria japonica (bachelor's buttons)
Kolkwitzia amabilis (beauty bush)
Philadelphus coronarius (mock orange)
Ribes sanguineum (flowering currant)
Spiraea arguta (bridal wreath)
Weigela florida (weigela)

BASIC PRUNING

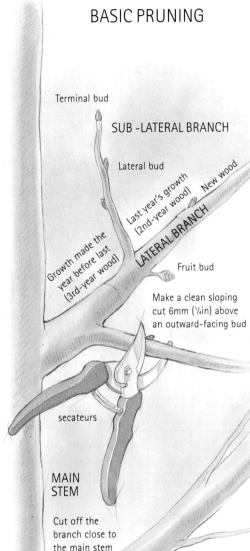

Terminal bud

SUB -LATERAL BRANCH

Lateral bud

Last year's growth (2nd-year wood)

New wood

Growth made the year before last (3rd-year wood)

LATERAL BRANCH

Fruit bud

Make a clean sloping cut 6mm (¼in) above an outward-facing bud

secateurs

MAIN STEM

Cut off the branch close to the main stem

handsaw

Cut the branch a quarter of the way through underneath before cutting from above

Chaenomeles x *superba* (japonica, Japanese quince) is a beautiful shrub with edible yellow fruits that benefits from summer pruning.

Ribes (flowering currant) is a compact, upright shrub that can also be pruned soon after flowering in late spring or early summer.

The acid-loving *Camellia* x *williamsii* 'Donation' can also be improved by pruning soon after flowering.

Training CLIMBERS

Climbing plants are very useful to give a garden a three-dimensional aspect, but they usually need to be properly supported and carefully trained for the best effect.

Wisteria is a dramatic and vigorous climber which is particularly good for framing archways or decorating pergolas.

MANY CLIMBERS make strong, even rampant growth through the summer months, and care needs to be taken that they don't get out of hand.

Plants climb in different ways. Some species are self-clinging and will attach themselves to any suitable support; they produce aerial roots or tendrils with adhesive pads at the tips, which fasten themselves to almost any rough surface. Other climbers have twining stems that thread their way through and around suitable supports, such as trellis work, stakes or tree trunks and branches; there are also

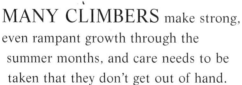

Passiflora caerulea (passionflower) is a showy creeper that climbs by means of tendrils.

species with tendrils that twist around the supports to hold the plant in place. Many of the best known climbers – clematis, sweet peas, grapevines, honeysuckle and wisteria – belong to this group. Finally, there are the plants which are more scramblers than true climbers; they produce long stems which grow over trees, shrubs, low walls and so on, but will tend to sprawl or trail rather than climb if left to their own devices.

Self-clinging climbers sound attractive because they are labour saving, but they have their drawbacks. When the plants are young, they often need some form of encouragement to get them started on their climb, in the

FIXING A TRELLIS TO A WALL
Rather than fixing the trellis directly to the wall, screw wooden battens or spacing blocks about 8cm (3in) thick to the wall and secure the trellis to these. This will maintain a flow of air behind the plant, leading to healthier growth.

form of canes or a small piece or trellis. Once they have gained a hold on the main support, however, they can be very difficult to remove. For this reason it is often a good idea to grow self-clinging climbers against a piece of

trellis supported away from a wall by battens, as described on the left.

Twining or tendril-clinging climbers need a suitable support to grow against or through. They can be effective when planted against a tree or large shrub and allowed to ramble through the branches; a piece of chicken wire or plastic wire wrapped around the tree trunk will give them a good start.

Against a wall or fence, grow twiners and scrambling plants on wooden or plastic trellis attached to 2.5cm (1in) wooden battens which hold it clear of the surface, or on a system of wires attached to vine eyes screwed into the wall (see below). In early summer, tie the young shoots gently to the support, using twine or plastic-coated wire ties secured in a figure-of-eight to avoid damage to the shoots. As they grow, they will support themselves on the wires or trellis work, but some continued training and tying in of some shoots may be necessary throughout the summer to ensure that they grow in the required direction to give a good, even coverage of the surface.

Rosa 'Schoolgirl' is a tall, upright climbing rose that flowers all through summer to autumn.

Clematis 'Nellie Moser' is a large-flowered, popular variety that adorns trellises throughout summer; it prefers partial shade.

FIXING WIRE TO WALLS
Plastic-covered wire stretched horizontally on a wall provides good support for climbers. Drill holes and screw vine eyes into them using pliers. Then thread and tighten the wire.

Humulus lupulus 'Aureus', the golden hop, is a vigorous herbaceous climber with twining growth. It fruits in late summer.

Trimming HEDGES

Hedge trimming is probably one of the least popular of summer tasks in the garden, but it is not a job that needs to be done very frequently – two or three times a year for a formal hedge, depending on its rate of growth, and once a year for an informal one will suffice.

ALTHOUGH hedge trimming can be hard work, there are plenty of ways to make the job easier.

Formal hedges are usually made from evergreen shrubs such as *Ligustrum ovalifolium* (privet), *Buxus sempervirens* (box), *Ilex aquifolium* (holly), *Taxus*

powered trimmer. Electric trimmers are lightweight and easy to use – when the hedge is within reach of a power socket – but great care needs to be taken to avoid cutting the flex.

Removing the clippings can be as much of a chore as the actual hedge

TRIMMING SHAPES
It is possible to trim your hedge into different shapes. An angled top (left) is aesthetically pleasing and helps the hedge shed snow; a rectangular wedge shape should always be trimmed evenly to prevent thinning.

Rosa 'Drummer Boy' is a bright cluster-flowered rose with a bushy habit. Like many rose bushes, it can be grown as an effective small barrier.

baccata (yew) and various other conifers such as *Thuja plicata* and *Chamaecyparis lawsoniana* (Lawson cypress). Deciduous subjects, such as *Carpinus betula* (hornbeam), *Fagus sylvatica* (beech) and *Crataegus monogyna* (hawthorn) can also form a good, close-clipped hedge. The timing of the first trim will vary with the type of hedge and the season, but usually falls at the beginning of summer, after nesting birds have raised their young.

While hedges can be cut with hand shears, it is very much easier to use a

cutting itself. Lay a tarpaulin or sheet of heavy-duty polythene at the base of the hedge before starting work, to catch the clippings and make clearing up much easier.

A low hedge – ideally around waist height – is much quicker and easier to trim than a taller one, but hedges are often used as screens against the weather or to provide privacy, when extra height is essential. Keep down the work by not growing the hedge any taller than is absolutely necessary. Cutting above head height with hand shears is very tiring – with powered trimmers it can also be dangerous.

A formal yew hedge is the perfect boundary, windbreak or divider for the larger garden. It requires regular attentive care.

Fagus sylvatica (beech) is an excellent hedging plant with foliage that changes from green to yellow in autumn and russet in winter.

Buxus sempervirens 'Marginata' (box) is a ubiquitous, slow-growing evergreen with a dense habit, ideal for edging beds or creating formal structures.

Chamaecyparis lawsoniana 'Allumii' (Lawson cypress) is a popular evergreen, good for creating a dense screen for privacy and as a windbreak.

trimmer. For the first cut of the year, a piece of string stretched taut between two canes will help you to achieve a straight top. The top of the hedge is often cut flat, like a table, or it may be cut in a rounded or apex shape. A flat top is not recommended in areas where snow is likely during the winter – rounded or pointed tops are better since they will shed the snow without deforming the hedge.

Informal hedges do not require so much work. Instead of being closely trimmed to give a smooth surface, the outline of the hedge is much freer and looser. Shears or powered trimmers can be used, but usually secateurs are all that is necessary to clip the hedge lightly back into shape. Hedges grown for their flowers, such as forsythia and berberis, are generally trimmed immediately after flowering; other informal hedges are cut as necessary during the summer to keep them within bounds.

Use a firm stepladder to reach the taller portions of the hedge.

Formal hedges should be trimmed to a wedge shape, slightly wider at the base than the top. This makes them more stable and helps to ensure that they do not become bare at the base. Start cutting at the base of the hedge and work up, cutting with an upward, sweeping motion when using a powered

Shrubs from CUTTINGS

As the summer progresses, shoots produced by shrubs earlier in the spring will begin to become firm and slightly more woody towards their base. These shoots make good propagating material, and cuttings made from them are known as semi-ripe or half-ripe cuttings.

Aucuba is a hardy, evergreen shrub; it is easily propagated from heeled cuttings 10–15cm (4–6in) long in late summer.

SEMI-RIPE cuttings can be taken from mid- to late summer. They do not root as quickly as softwood cuttings, but they are less delicate and less likely to suffer severe wilting. Compost should be prepared as for softwood cuttings; a proprietary seed and cuttings compost containing some sharp sand is ideal. Use trays or pots for the cuttings, filling them with moist compost, striking the compost off level with a piece of wood and firming it before topping it with a layer of sand.

Take the cuttings from the parent plants preferably in the morning of a fairly cool, overcast day. Choose sideshoots that are just beginning to ripen and become darker at their base; either cut the shoots with secateurs, or if they are an appropriate length, pull them gently from the main stem, leaving a little 'heel' of bark at their base.

Most cuttings are trimmed to around 10cm (4in) long. Remove the lower leaves and cut the base straight across immediately below a leaf node, using a sharp knife; if heel cuttings are used, just trim the heel of bark lightly.

TAKING SEMI-RIPE CUTTINGS
Shrubs are a good source for semi-ripe cuttings. (1) Tear a long side-shoot away from the main stem with a heel of the old wood. (2) Neatly trim the base of the cutting and dip it in hormone rooting powder or gel. (3) Insert the cutting into a prepared tray of compost covered with sand.

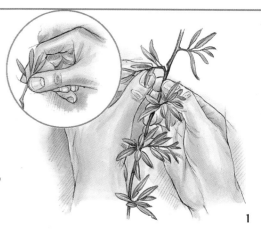

1

2

3

Semi-ripe cuttings do not root as quickly as

Berberis thunbergii atropurpurea is a deciduous shrub suitable for smaller gardens which can be easily propagated from semi-ripe cuttings.

Escallonia 'Apple Blossom' can be propagated by means of half-ripe cuttings and is a durable, self-regenerating plant often used as a windbreak.

It is not just semi-ripe cuttings that can be taken at this time of year. Plants such as dianthus continue to provide suitable shoots for softwood cuttings all through the summer months.

Rooting hormone compounds are of more use on semi-ripe cuttings than softwood ones. When the base of the cutting has been dipped in the powder, it should be tapped on the side of the container several times to leave a light film of powdert. Insert the cuttings into the compost and firm them in; water lightly with a fine rose on the can.

The ideal place for semi-ripe cuttings to spend the winter is in a cold frame. Keep them just moist and ventilate the frame in warm weather, but protect the cuttings from frost. If a cold frame is not available, a frost-free greenhouse, unheated room in the home or even a garden shed or garage can be used. In autumn, deciduous cuttings will shed their leaves, which should be cleared away to prevent them rotting. As spring approaches, bring the cuttings into a light location. Once the cuttings have rooted and are starting to grow away from the tips, pot them up individually and plant them out in the garden as soon as they are large enough to survive outdoors.

Ilex x altaclarensis 'Golden King' – a variety of common holly – also responds well to propagation by semi-ripe cuttings.

softwood cuttings, but are tougher

Summer-sown VEGETABLES

Although the main sowing period in the kitchen garden is in spring, there are quite a number of crops that can be sown in the summer months. Some of these are fast-maturing crops which will be ready for harvest by autumn; others are for winter or spring.

HEAT AND DROUGHT can cause difficulties for summer sowing. Some seeds, such as lettuce, become dormant in high temperatures and refuse to germinate. Other crops will germinate, but the seedlings run immediately to seed almost before any leaves have formed. It is important to choose the right varieties for sowing at this time of year; any good seed catalogue will contain the information you need to help you choose.

The following crops can all be sown in the summer months.

Beetroot Choose a fast-maturing baby beet such as the F_1 hybrid 'Action'. Sow seeds thinly in rows and thin to around 10–15cm (4–6in).

Calabrese Calabrese is a popular type of broccoli which forms a large, central green head that will be followed by smaller sideshoots once it has been cut. Sow two or three calabrese seeds at each station, spacing them 15–23cm (6–9in) apart and thin to the strongest seedling. The varieties 'Christmas Marvel' and 'Autumn Spear' can both be sown in early summer.

Carrots Sow quick-maturing carrots such as 'Nanco', 'Rocket' and 'Amsterdam Forcing' thinly in shallow drills from early to midsummer. Sowing in summer instead of spring helps avoid damage by carrot root fly.

Chinese cabbage This cabbage can be used cooked or raw in salads. Sow from early to late summer, thinning seedlings to 30cm (12in) apart. 'Ruffles' is a popular variety.

Florence fennel Aniseed flavoured, like the leafy herb fennel, Florence fennel has broad leaf bases which make a swollen

Nothing is as satisfying for the keen gardener as a flourishing kitchen garden, packed with rows of tasty beans, onions, curly kale, carrots and salad crops.

'bulb' in warm weather. Sow in high summer, thinning to 20cm (8in) apart.

French beans Sow seeds 15cm (6in) apart in early and midsummer. 'Masterpiece' and 'Primel' are among many suitable varieties.

Japanese onions Sow seed in late summer to mature the following midsummer. 'Senshyu Semi-Globe Yellow' and 'Imae Early Yellow' are reliable varieties.

Kohl rabi Turnip-flavoured swollen stems that should be eaten when they are the size of tennis balls. Sow from early to late summer, thinning seedlings to 15cm (6in) apart. 'Rowel' and 'Lanro' have white

flesh, 'Purple Danube' and 'Purple Vienna' purple, as the name suggests.

Lettuce Sow small amounts of seed for succession through to midsummer, selecting varieties such as 'All The Year Round' and the quick-growing 'Fortune'. Water the drills before sowing and sow in the cool of evening. For winter and spring lettuce, sow 'Arctic King' or 'Valdor' outside in late summer and early autumn.

Radish Summer radish varieties can be sown until early autumn but keep them watered to prevent woodiness. Winter radish is sown from midsummer to mid-autumn.

Spinach Spinach is daylength sensitive and will bolt if sown in early summer. Sow varieties such as 'Longstanding' and 'Vivat' from late summer for an autumn crop.

Spring cabbage Sow in a seedbed in mid- and late summer to plant out in early and mid-autumn for a spring crop. 'Pixie' and 'Spring Hero' are good varieties. Spring greens can be sown where they are to crop in mid- and late summer for leafy greens in autumn or spring.

Turnips Sow fast-maturing baby turnips such as 'Tiny Pal' and 'Tokyo Cross' in late summer for harvest in early winter, or sow seed in late summer to be harvested as green turnip tops in spring.

Brassica cernua (Chinese cabbage) is a quick-growing plant, that looks similar to cos lettuce. Sow seeds in the ground in midsummer for cutting in early autumn.

Sow globe varieties of beetroot from late spring to midsummer. As soon as they are large enough, lift them carefully with a fork, since damaged roots will bleed.

The dense, round heads of small-growing spring cabbage, sown in late summer, are ready for cutting young from late autumn onwards.

Summer Care of VEGETABLES

Succulent summer crops of peppers, aubergines, courgettes and tomatoes are the result of careful attention to their cultivation and to the eradication of weeds and pests.

The vegetable garden should be well filled during the summer months, with crops at all stages of growth.

AT THIS TIME of year, there are successional sowings still to be made, earlier-sown seedlings to be cared for, maturing plants to be fed and watered and crops to be harvested.

Seedling care Vegetable seedlings should be kept free from weeds as far as possible, but take care when using a hoe between the rows. Thin seedlings out to the correct spacing as soon as they are large enough.

Successional sowings Continue to sow crops to give an extended harvest – see pages 80–81 for which types to sow. As the summer progresses, it may be necessary to choose varieties that can cope with the weather conditions.

Harvest summer vegetables frequently for the largest crops and longest season

Watering and feeding In dry weather, concentrate watering on those crops that will benefit most – leafy vegetables, plants in flower (such as peas and beans), newly transplanted subjects and germinating seedlings. Apply sufficient water to penetrate the soil to root level. Give leafy crops an application of high-nitrogen fertilizer to boost growth; a liquid feed is absorbed most rapidly.

Pest problems As vegetable crops develop, so more pests will put in an appearance.

Combat pests by checking plants for problems regularly and taking action as soon as trouble is spotted. Simple measures often work well – for example, washing aphids off runner

Staking and training Provide supports for crops that need them as early as possible, before the plants become tangled up with each other (see below).

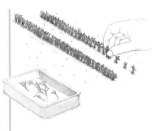

PLANTING RUNNER BEANS
When planting out runner beans that have been raised in pots, keep the rootball intact. Set a plant at the foot of each support and water it. The beans will soon twine around the pole.

Earthing up Plants such as potatoes, leeks, celery and Florence fennel will all benefit from being earthed up. Draw up soil carefully around the base of the plants with a hoe, a little at a time over the summer months, being careful not to bury plants too deeply or damage the stems while you are doing it.

More carrot seeds will germinate than can be left to grow, so they must be thinned. Choose a dull, damp evening, water the plants, then thin them to 4–5cm (1½–2in) apart. Remove the thinnings – their smell will attract carrot fly.

beans with a jet of water, pinching out blackfly infested tips of broad beans as soon as they have set their pods, and breaking off and destroying outer leaves of cabbage or lettuce where early mealy aphid infestations are seen.

Harvesting Some vegetables are harvested while they are young and tender, others are left to maturity – it depends on the type and variety of vegetables grown. Harvest frequently for the largest crops and longest season of production.

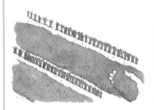

Bury the thinnings under other matter in the compost heap. Spreading lawn mowings between the rows, will also help to deter carrot fly – these pests are most likely to attack if the soil is dry.

TRAINING VEGETABLES
Peas usually appreciate twiggy sticks or netting or an arrangement of canes and string; runner and climbing french beans will grow up netting or canes arranged in wigwams or as an A-frame. Once the young shoots of beans have been guided in the right direction they will soon twine round and attach themselves to the supports.

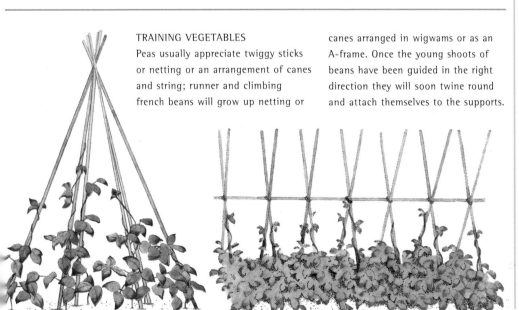

Carrot fly are attracted by the smell of the plants, and hanging strips of old cloth soaked in paraffin above the crop is an excellent way to keep them away from the seedlings.

Growing HERBS

Herbs are valuable plants for every garden – even the smallest plot. Because herbs have intense flavours, only small numbers of plants need to be grown, and as well as being useful in the kitchen, they are attractive and interesting into the bargain.

A mixed herb garden offers both visual interest and a valuable source of culinary flavourings.

Agastache foeniculum (giant hyssop), with its bold spikes of purplish flowers, is a good border plant. Add its aniseed-flavoured leaves to salads.

DEDICATED HERB gardens are popular features, though it is by no means essential to grow herbs like this.

Herb gardens often take on distinct geometric patterns such as chequerboards, or circular beds divided into equal-sized segments – probably derived from the old-fashioned knot gardens which were so popular in Elizabethan times. Most of these formal designs rely on symmetry for much of their effect, and this can be difficult to maintain, since different herbs have widely differing growth habits. A less formal style of

herb garden is usually more appropriate for the majority of gardeners. Here herbs can be grown in groups of varying colours, forms and sizes, in schemes of mixed contrasts and complements.

A herb can be loosely defined as a 'useful plant', and though today they are mainly grown for cooking, they are also used medicinally. Most herbs have aromatic leaves, though stems, roots, flowers and seeds may also be used.

It is in the summer months that herbs and herb gardens really come into their own. The warm sun brings out the fragrance of many of the plants. Some

Rosmarinus officinalis (rosemary) is an intensely aromatic evergreen herb that makes an initially dense bush. Its attractive blue flowers are an added bonus.

Borago officinalis (borage) is an annual herb with beautiful flowers which are used to decorate summer dishes, salads, pickles and punches.

HERB TROUGH

Herbs are perfect for container growing and, if picked reasonably sparingly, will provide sprigs for use in the kitchen over an extended season. There are plenty of contrasting herbs to provide visual interest.

herbs need to be brushed past or their foliage squeezed gently for their fragrance to be released; others scent the air around them freely on warm days. By early to midsummer they have made sufficient new growth to enable sprigs to be harvested for use, and later in the season it is possible to gather bunches of herbs for drying or freezing for the winter.

The majority of aromatic culinary herbs originate from warm Mediterranean countries and appreciate an open, sunny but sheltered position in the garden. Most demand a free-draining soil; a few will grow well in moist soil, but others will soon rot in damp conditions, particularly if they are also in the shade.

Some herbs can be planted in the cracks in paving or in dry stone walls, as well as in the garden; positioning them where they will be brushed against will ensure their fragrance is regularly released. Most herbs are also ideal for containers, which can be moved around the garden as desired.

Container-grown herbs can be planted throughout the summer. Prepare the soil for them by digging it over and incorporating some sand or fine grit unless it is already very free draining. Turn the herbs out of their pots and plant them firmly; many will appreciate a topdressing of grit immediately round the stems after planting. Water carefully to leave the soil evenly moist, not wet.

Thymus x *citriodorus* 'Silver Queen' (variegated lemon thyme) is a small, hardy, evergreen shrub, widely used in cooking.

Selecting the BEST HERBS

There are many herbs which are both easy to grow and widely used in the kitchen. The following selection will be appreciated for their looks as well as for their flavour and fragrance.

Shrubby common sage is a semi-evergreen whose strong-flavoured leaves are good with pork and duck. Purple and red-leaved varieties also exist.

Basil *Ocimum basilicum*
A half-hardy annual with oval, pointed, rather soft leaves of a light green and a warm, spicy, clove-like fragrance. Basil is indispensable for Italian dishes and particularly good with tomatoes. Sow seeds when all risk of frost is over.

Bay *Laurus nobilis*
One of the few herbs that will form a tree. It is an evergreen, only moderately hardy, with deep green, pointed, leathery leaves which have undulating margins. The leaves are torn before use to release their distinctive, warm fragrance.

Chives *Allium schoenoprasum*
An herbaceous perennial which forms large clumps of deep green, grassy,

Certain plants of the antennaria family were once used as medicines, but are now grown for their ornamental value.

Chives   Mint   Fennel

hollow leaves which have a mild onion flavour. In summer, rounded pompom heads of papery, pale purple, edible flowers are produced. Use the chopped leaves in a variety of cooked dishes or raw, along with the flowers, in salads.

Fennel *Foeniculum vulgare*

A tall perennial with dainty, finely cut, thread-like leaves whose strong aniseed scent associates particularly well with fish. Umbels of yellow flowers are produced at the tops of the stems, and the ribbed seeds that follow them are also aromatic and can be used in cooking.

Marjoram *Origanum vulgare*

A low-growing herbaceous perennial with oval leaves. 'Aureum' (golden marjoram) has golden-yellow leaves.

Parsley

Mint *Mentha* species

A well-known herb with pointed or rounded, toothed leaves and square stems. Apple mint and peppermint are among the best culinary varieties.

Parsley *Petroselinum crispum*

Another very well-known herb. The common, crisply curled variety is attractive as an edging plant, but flat-leaved parsley is better for salads and Mediterranean dishes.

Rosemary *Rosmarinus officinalis*

An evergreen shrub with needle-like, silver-backed leaves and hooded, pale blue flowers in spring and summer. Leaves are strongly aromatic and have a wide range of culinary and therapeutic uses.

Tarragon *Artemisia dracunculus*

A half-hardy perennial with slender, deep green leaves which have an aromatic, aniseed fragrance.

Thyme *Thymus* species

Low-growing sub-shrubs with very small, aromatic leaves, good for planting in cracks in paving. There are lots of different species and varieties of thyme with variegated or coloured leaves and a range of scents, including lemon and caraway. Pink, purple or white flowers are very attractive to bees.

Winter savory *Satureja montana*

A small evergreen shrub with deep green, narrow leaves. Their warm aroma is traditionally associated with beans of all types.

Laurus nobilis (bay laurel, sweet bay) is widely used in cooking casseroles and other meat dishes.

Ocimum basilicum (basil) comes in several different varieties including bush, sweet and lemon basil.

Salvia officinalis (common sage) has many culinary and medicinal uses.

Protecting Fruit from BIRDS

Home-grown fruit, picked and eaten straight from the tree, is one of the major pleasures of summer for gardeners. Unfortunately, wild birds share our enthusiasm for fresh fruit, and some form of bird protection is usually necessary if we are to salvage any of the crop for our own use.

BLACKBIRDS AND members of the thrush family are major culprits when it comes to damaging fruit. They are particularly keen on soft fruit, with currants, raspberries, strawberries and blueberries especially prone to attack. Birds are not as particular as we may

Birds are difficult pests to deal with... keep them away by netting your crops!

be about waiting for soft fruit to ripen, which means they usually beat us to it when it comes to harvesting. Later in the summer, apples and pears are also attacked, although the birds usually wait until these fruits are moderately ripe and soft enough to eat. Individual apples and pears may show only a small amount of damage from pecking, but it is enough to start the fruits rotting, and makes them useless for storage.

Netting and fruit cages

Birds are difficult pests to deal with, and the most reliable method of preventing damage is to keep them away by netting the crops. Where large amounts of fruit are grown in one place, a fruit cage is a reliable, if

expensive, answer. Large fruit cages are convenient because they have ample headroom and access for picking and caring for the crop. Small-scale fruit cages can be constructed around smaller groups of plants or individual bushes. Aluminium poles or wooden or plastic supports should hold the netting clear of the crop; this is important, because if netting is simply draped over the branches, birds can still peck the fruit through the mesh. Strawberries, raspberries and currants are relatively easy to protect in this way; tree fruit is more difficult unless the trees are trained against a wall or fence.

Other deterrents

Where netting is not practical, gardeners must rely on bird deterrents. Chemical

It is easy to make your own basic fruit cage, especially up against a wall.

(Right) A bird-scarer in the form of a cat's face sometimes makes an effective deterrent.

Summer

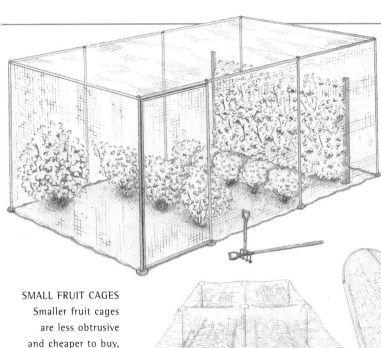

LARGE FRUIT CAGES
Large-scale fruit cages are probably the most effective deterrent against scavenging birds, but they tend to be very expensive and take up a lot of room in the garden.

Blackberries, raspberries and loganberries all belong to the same family. Of the three, blackberries are least likely to be attacked by birds.

SMALL FRUIT CAGES
Smaller fruit cages are less obtrusive and cheaper to buy, but access for the gardener is restricted and difficult.

Raspberries are irresistible to wild birds, their colour making them easy to spot. Netting is the best form of protection.

deterrents are only of use for protecting buds in the winter – they rely on their unpleasant taste, which rules them out for use on the fruit itself. Other common deterrents include loud noises and flashing or sparkling objects designed to scare the birds away. Unfortunately, birds tend to become accustomed to these startling objects after a short time, and they lose their effectiveness.

The explosive bird scarers used commercially are not suitable for garden use, but humming line – plastic tape stretched taut between posts, which vibrates and hums in the wind – is sometimes successful. Tape from old, unwanted video and audio cassettes can

be used instead of proprietary products. Various glittering and sparkling bird-scaring devices can be bought, or improvised at home. Aluminium foil (milk bottle tops were an old favourite) can be scrunched up and threaded on strings hung around the trees, and unwanted compact discs can be strung up in a similar way to flash in the sun as they twist and turn. Children's windmills are another option – they provide noise as well as movement. There are a number of devices which mimic the appearance of bird predators. These need to be moved around the garden regularly to have any chance of success.

The large-fruited loganberry is another favourite with birds, which will severely reduce crops is they are allowed to.

The Soft FRUIT HARVEST

The soft fruit season usually begins in the garden with strawberries towards the end of early summer. Next on the scene are the raspberries, and from midsummer onwards, currants and gooseberries. Blackberries and blueberries mark the end of the summer season, along with autumn-fruiting raspberries.

The summer soft fruit harvest brings an abundance of tasty treats to the kitchen and dining table.

Black currants Black currants are carried in small, pendent bunches known as 'strigs'. The berries nearest the main stem are the first to ripen, turning from pink to a deep blue-black; those at the tip of the strig ripen a few days later. Individual berries can be picked as they are ready, but it is much quicker to harvest the whole strig once most of the berries on it are sufficiently ripe. Strigs can be stored on absorbent paper in the crisper of the refrigerator for a few days; for longer storage, fruits are frozen, bottled or turned into jam. Black currants can be eaten raw or cooked.

Blackberries Early varieties ripen in late summer and the season extends into early or mid-autumn. Choose a dry day to pick the fruits when they have turned from red to black, pulling them gently from the cane and removing the calyx if necessary. Cultivated thornless varieties are less painful to pick than the prickly types. Spread the fruits in a single layer on absorbent paper and store in the refrigerator for two or three days, or freeze or turn into preserves. Ripe berries can be eaten raw, but blackberries are more commonly cooked.

Pick soft fruits on a warm, dry day, as

Summer

Blueberries Ripe blueberries are a rich, deep blue-black colour, but they are covered with a fine bloom which makes them appear lighter blue. Wait until the fruits are not just blue but soft before picking them individually. They can be stored in the refrigerator for up to ten days. They are most delicious eaten fresh but are also good cooked in pies and puddings.

Gooseberries Culinary gooseberries, which are cooked before eating, are picked green, as soon as they are large enough, and will keep for a week or so in the refrigerator. 'Top and tail'

gooseberries carefully before cooking or eating, using a small sharp knife to avoid sore fingers.

Raspberries Raspberries are ready for picking when the fruits are soft and juicy and a deep pink colour all over. A good test is to see whether the fruit pulls away from the plug cleanly, leaving the plug on the cane; those which will not come away from the plug are not quite ripe.

Red and white currants Like black currants, fruit is carried in strigs and is shiny and jewel-like when ripe. Both red and white currants are nearly always cooked before eating and are much more 'pippy' than blackcurrants. Their flavour is pleasantly sharp. They are often used in preserves.

Strawberries Beds need to be checked over daily once ripening has started; pick the strawberries when the tip of the fruit has turned from white to red. Pick by pinching the stem, keeping the calyx and plug intact – once the plug is removed, the fruit will soon rot. Remove damaged or rotting fruits as you find them to prevent any infection spreading. Eat strawberries as soon after harvest as possible; sound fruits can be kept in the crisper of the refrigerator for a day or two only. Jam is the traditional way to deal with a glut.

Pick soft fruit with the greatest of care; it is easy to squash and damage the berries.

damp fruit will quickly go mouldy

Black currants are a versatile fruit with many different culinary uses. They can be eaten either raw or cooked.

Gooseberries come in many different varieties. Most need cooking before they are palatable enough to eat, although some dessert varieties can be eaten raw.

Blueberries are difficult to grow in abundance, but they are a pleasant soft fruit with a distinctive flavour.

Strawberry CULTIVATION

You should plant strawberries in mid- or late summer, giving the plants time to establish themselves before they carry a crop the following year. For the best results start with young plants.

A LIGHT, free-draining soil and an open, sunny, sheltered position suit strawberries best. You should avoid planting them in a frost pocket – their flowers are very prone to frost damage, and a late frost could destroy much of the crop. Prepare a bed for strawberries by digging the soil thoroughly and incorporating as much well-rotted organic matter (such as farmyard manure and garden compost) as you can. Remove all perennial weeds – these are a real nuisance in a strawberry bed.

As strawberries are prone to virus diseases, which can reduce yields severely, you should buy only certified virus-free plants. This does not mean that they will not succumb to viruses once they are planted in your garden (viruses are spread by aphids), but at least it means you are starting off with plants that are guaranteed to be healthy. Strawberries for summer planting are supplied as either bare-root runners or growing in pots. The earliest available plants will be cold-stored runners. These will have been lifted during the winter and refrigerated until planting time, in midsummer. Cold-stored runners will give a higher yield in their first year than ordinary pot-

Keeping the strawberry plants clear of pests will result in plump fruit and a generous harvest.

grown runners, which usually only become available from late summer.

Strawberry plants should be spaced at 30–45cm (12–18in) in rows about 90cm (36in) apart. Dig a hole in the prepared soil with a trowel, making sure that it is deep enough for the runner to be planted with the crown just at soil level. Push the soil back against the roots of the plant with the trowel and press it in it well with the sole of your boot – strawberries must

Strawberry plants can be easily propagated by spreading out and pegging down the runners. When they have rooted, cut them off from the mother plant.

to root them to provide new plants (see illustration on page 92).

When the crop has been picked, the plants should be treated rather drastically. You should cutt off and remove all of the foliage, along with the straw, and

Strawberries like a light, free-draining soil and an open, sunny, sheltered position

burn them. This helps to control pests and diseases andalso allows the new leaves to develop. It is important not to cut the foliage too low – you should leave about 10cm (4in)so that the crowns of the plants, where new leaves are forming, are not damaged. You can use a pair of shears or a nylon line trimmer. A traditional method was to set fire to the straw on a dry day but this is more difficult to control and may not be popular with your neighbours. Clearing the old leaves should be done as soon as possible after picking has finished, preferably within a day or two, otherwise there is too much risk of damage to the crowns of the plants.

be planted firmly. Water if necessary after planting. Sometimes flowers will form on cold-stored runners shortly after planting, and these should be pinched off.

Summer care of established strawberries

In early summer, as the berries begin to swell, strawberries should be strawed down if this has not already been done (see page 47). This will protect the fruit from soil splashes and damage by slugs. Runners should be removed regularly as they form, unless you want

Alpine strawberry plants are easy to grow and can be raised from seed. Fruits are very small and rather dry, but they have an intense strawberry flavour.

It is easy to root replacement plants from runners pegged down into pots, but remember that these may already be affected by virus diseases. If you decide to replace the whole bed at once, by buying-in certified stock, remake the bed in a place where strawberry plants have not been grown for several years.

Pruning TRAINED FRUIT

Trained forms of fruit trees are ideal for smaller gardens, enabling a variety of fruit to be grown where there is not the space for full-size trees.

THE OBVIOUS WAY to control the size of trees is to prune them. However, pruning in the dormant season encourages strong, vigorous growth to be made the following year. Vigorous growth is certainly not desirable for restricted forms of fruit, so the main pruning of these takes place in the summer. Summer pruning slows down leafy growth, and encourages the formation of fruit.

Apples and pears

Trained apples and pears are usually grown either as cordons or espaliers, flat against a wall or trellis supported by a system of posts and wires. Cordons are single stems; espaliers' branches are trained in single or multiple parallel horizontal rows. Cordons are easier to maintain and allow more trees to be planted in a given space. Summer pruning methods for established cordons and espaliers is the same.

Pruning method Pruning of apples and pears starts in midsummer. Stems to be pruned are laterals (sideshoots), which should be about as thick as a pencil and starting to become woody at their base. At the bottom of each shoot is a group of three or so leaves growing closely

Heavy crops of apples often consist of small fruits. Reducing the number of buds and thinning out small fruits will give a more satisfactory crop of fewer but larger apples.

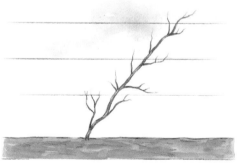

TRAINED FRUIT FORMS: CORDONS
These are single-stemmed trees, usually grown at an angle of 45 degrees. When planting cordons, make sure that the grafting point remains above soil level, to prevent the grafted variety from rooting.

ESPALIERS
For an espaliered tree, suitable branches are trained horizontally to form a tree with a central stem and regular tiers of branches about 45cm (18in) apart. Espaliered trees require plenty of space.

A trained espalier is a good way to grow either apples or pears, but it will require constant maintenance in order to flourish.

together; this is the basal cluster. Above this cluster the leaves are more widely spaced along the stem, and it is these leaves that are counted when deciding where to make pruning cuts.

Laterals which have grown directly from the main stem in the current season are cut back to three leaves above the basal cluster. Some new shoots will also have grown from existing sideshoots, and these should be pruned back even harder, to one leaf above the basal cluster. This encourages spurs – groups of short, knobbly stems which bear fruit buds – to form.

Carry out summer pruning over a number of weeks, pruning back shoots as soon as they reach a suitable size. Spreading out the pruning prevents it being too much of a shock to the tree.

Plums and cherries

These fruits make an attractive feature when grown as a fan trained on wires against a wall or fence.

Pruning method During early summer, new shoots that are needed to fill in the framework of the tree should be selected and tied into place. Any other new shoots which are not required should be cut back to six leaves from the base in midsummer, reducing them to three leaves from the base in late summer, after the fruit has been picked.

Prune cordons every year in late spring, cutting off the tip of the main stem of the cordon, leaving about 1cm ($\frac{1}{2}$in) of new wood. Tie the stem to its support.

In midsummer, when laterals (sideshoots on the main stem) are about 23cm (9in) long, cut them back to the third leaf above the basal cluster. On sub-laterals, cut above the first leaf beyond the basal cluster.

STEPOVERS
The ultimate in small trees, the stepover is an espaliered tree with just one tier of branches. It can be grown as an edging to a bed and will bear a small crop of fruit.

FANS
Cherry trees are perhaps the most commonly found fan-trained trees. They are normally grown against a wall or fence, with the branches spread out in a regular fan shape and the tree kept flat against the wall.

Looking After THE LAWN

A well-kept lawn forms a centrepiece to the garden which is both practical and a visual delight. This lawn sets off the well-stocked borders perfectly.

A healthy lawn enhances every aspect of the garden, particularly in high summer, when its cool greenness provides the perfect contrast to brightly coloured flowers.

LAWNS NEED regular attention to keep them in trim and in good health during the summer.

Mowing In early summer, lawns must be mown at least once a week. As long as the blades are set to the right height, it is impossible to harm a lawn by mowing it too often – it is mowing too closely that does the damage. The ideal mowing height depends on the type of grass, but you should not cut off more than one-third of the length of the grass (see pages 34–35). Cutting too close weakens the grass and makes it more susceptible to drought.

As long as mowing is carried out frequently, the clippings will be short enough to leave on the lawn. They will decompose, returning nutrients to the soil and reducing the need for fertilizing 'Mulching mowers' chop the clippings very small, so they decompose quickly.

Edging After each mowing, trim the lawn edges with shears to keep them looking neat, but be careful not to tread on them clumsily, since in dry weather they become crumbly and are easily damaged. Remove long clippings from the soil; short clippings can be left, since they will soon wither away. Edges should be recut with a half-moon edging iron once a year in spring; any repairs to damage are best left until autumn.

Weeding A selective weedkiller will deal with broad-leaved weeds in grass and, if it has not been used in spring, it can be applied in early summer (see pages 36–37). Dispose of grass clippings for the first two or three mowings after selective weedkiller treatment – do not put them on a compost heap or use them as a mulch, since the weedkiller they contain may damage garden plants.

Feeding To remain in good condition a lawn needs a regular top-up of nutrients; in spring and summer, nitrogen is most in demand. It is responsible for lush, leafy growth and a rich green colour. Water in powder and granule fertilizers if rain has not fallen

1   2   3   4

DIFFERENT TYPES OF LAWNMOWER

There are several types of lawnmower in common usage. These are: (1) Push mower. This type of mower is suitable only for small lawns. (2) Petrol cylinder mower. This is probably the most popular type of mower and certainly the best for larger lawns. (3) Wheeled rotary mower. This type of mower is ideal for cutting rough grass. (4) Hover rotary mower. This type can be electric or petrol-engined. Both are easy to use.

within two days of application; in dry conditions a liquid fertilizer, applied through a hose-end dilutor, is better.

Watering To keep a lawn green and attractive in dry spells, it is necessary to water it. Water wisely to avoid waste (see pages 60–63), and do all you can to improve the drought resistance of the grass by not cutting it too short, fertilizing it regularly and leaving the clippings on the surface. On free-draining soils, topdress the lawn with bulky organic matter in autumn.

In summer, lawns usually need watering after 7–10 days without rain, although this varies according to soil conditions, type of grass and the general weather conditions. If the grass springs back up when you walk across the lawn, watering is not needed; if it becomes upright slowly or only partially, it is starting to feel the effects of water shortage, and you need to start doing some watering.

Do not water grass little and often, but give it a thorough soaking that will reach down to the lowest roots. A lawn sprinkler is the most efficient method of watering. Apply between 1–2.5cm (½–1in) of water at a time. If you are not sure how much you are applying, place one or two straight-sided containers, such as empty jam jars or tin cans, under the area covered by the sprinkler and measure the depth of water that collects in the bottom.

Lawn weeds can spoil the overall effect of what is often the centrepiece of the garden. Because weeds are extremely hardy and reproduce rapidly they are more efficient than most grasses at taking nutrients and water from the soil and, left unchecked, will literally starve a lawn. Use a selective weedkiller when necessary, and where just a few weeds are present, dig out individual plants or spot-weed with a specially formulated hand-sprayer, sponge or wax-based stick.

Aegopodium podagraria (ground elder) is an extremely invasive perennial, once established.

Equisetum arvense (common horsetail) is another vigorous, persistent lawn weed.

Maintaining Flower BORDERS

The summer garden is, for many people, all about flowers. The role of the gardener is to display the flowers to their best advantage, and keep the show going as long as possible.

WHILE FOLIAGE plants play a valuable and attractive role, it is usually as a backdrop to the bright colours and complex forms of the many different types of blooms that are at their peak through the summer months. It is up to the gardener to maintain this balance.

Deadheading As flowers on perennials begin to fade, they should be removed, either by pinching them off with a finger and thumb or cutting them with secateurs. Not only does it improve the appearance of the plants, but it prevents plants wasting energy in setting seed, and helps to encourage further flowers to be produced, extending the season. The only exceptions are where plants are valuable for their seedheads – *Lunaria* (honesty), *Papaver* (poppies) or *Physalis* (Chinese lanterns), for example.

Some plants can be cut back rather harder after blooming. The old flowering stems of early-flowering delphiniums and lupins can be cut out to ground level, and new shoots growing at the base may have time to produce another flush of flowers before the end of the summer.

Supporting Perennials should be regularly tied in to their supports during the summer months. A summer thunderstorm or high winds can flatten insecurely supported plants and ruin their shape. Where stems have been flattened or blown about, they should be picked up and retied as soon as possible – their growth starts to become misshapen and distorted within a few hours.

Watering One of the beauties of an established perennial border is that plants are usually drought resistant,

(Above) Tall-growing, annual cosmos provide bright colour in the border.

(Right) *Tagetes* 'Starfire Mix' flower spectacularly throughout the summer.

Flag irises should be lifted and divided in early summer, just after flowering. Discard worn-out parts of the rhizome and replant healthy sections with fresh leaves and plenty of roots.

Kniphofia rooperi (red hot poker) is a striking plant, producing bold flower spikes late in the season. It needs full sun and well-drained soil. Yellow and white varieties also exist.

Anemone x *hybrida* 'Queen Charlotte' (Japanese anemone) is a popular variety, flowering late in the season. It forms large clumps in good soil and prefers sun or partial shade.

Helenium 'Golden Youth' (sneezewort) produces bright yellow flowers late in the season. Mulch this plant in spring and keep it well watered. It may require staking, since it can grow to 90cm (36in).

Papaver orientale 'Turkish Delight' (oriental poppy) has large flowers with crinkled petals in mid-season, followed by untidy foliage. It needs well-drained, sunny soil.

and watering is rarely necessary. In early summer, however, watering may be needed for recently planted specimens, and in really dry spells, all perennials will appreciate a thorough watering which makes sure the soil is moist right down at root level.

Feeding Perennials do not need much in the way of fertilizer – in fact, an excess of high-nitrogen fertilizer will encourage lush leafy growth at the expense of flowers.

Annuals Herbaceous perennials are not the only plants to provide summer colour from flowers – hardy annuals can give a long-lasting display, too. They need similar treatment to perennials in that they should be regularly deadheaded and provided with supports where necessary; slender canes or short, twiggy sticks are usually most suitable. It is not too late to sow more hardy annuals – those sown in early and midsummer will extend the flowering season right into early autumn.

Plants for SUMMER (1)

When the ornamental garden is in full bloom at the height of summer, gardening can almost feel easy. It is as if nature has saved all her best efforts for one, all too often brief, season.

A sumptuous summer border repays the effort that the gardener puts in all year round.

Centaurea cyanus (cornflower) comes in many different colours and is excellent for cutting.

SUMMER IS the season of plenty in the ornamental garden – there are almost too many plants to mention. While there are numerous brightly coloured blooms to enjoy from border plants, annuals and biennials, don't forget to use plant foliage to tone down the display and provide an effective, cooling contrast. While bold, bright colours are always popular, the cooler white, blue and pastel shades can form a restful oasis in the summer garden.

Plants are not only valuable for their looks. Summer is the time when we really appreciate fragrance in the garden, whether it is from flowers or foliage. The lovely white blooms of *Philadelphus* are called mock orange because of the resemblance of their fragrance to that of orange blossom; 'Belle Etoile' and 'Innocence' are good single varieties, while 'Glacier' is late flowering with fully double blooms.

Roses are always popular, and while not every variety is scented, many are. The old-fashioned shrub roses have particularly rich perfumes, 'Madame Isaac Pereire', 'Boule de Neige' and 'Madame Hardy' among them. A longer flowering season can be had from the

Summer is the season of plenty in the garden

Summer

Eschscholzia 'Thai Silk Mixed' (Californian poppy) is an annual suitable for rock gardens and paving.

Lavandula angustifolia (lavender) is a fragrant, abundant summer plant that thrives in dry conditions.

Rosa 'Gloire de Dijon' is an old-fashioned Victorian climber. Its large flowers offer sweet scent all summer. Train it against a wall in a warm, sheltered spot.

many modern English roses, bred to have all the good points of old-fashioned types without their faults.

Lavender is another plant well loved for its scent, released from the opening flower buds by a gentle squeeze.

Lavandula angustifolia 'Hidcote' is one of the most popular varieties; 'Munstead' is slightly more compact, with intensely blue flowers. Honeysuckle, with its red and white or yellow trumpets, competes with white-flowered jasmine to be the most sweetly scented climber; Dianthus (border pinks), Nicotiana (sweet tobacco flowers), lilies, peonies and heliotrope are just a few of the other flowers contributing to the fragrant delights of the border.

Rosa 'Fragrant Cloud' is a small, upright, large-flowered rose with particularly vigorous growth. It has a delightful fragrance.

Rosa 'Frühlingsgold' has wonderful large, semidouble blooms that appear early in the season. A beautifully fragrant rose.

The purple spires of Salvia 'Victoria' are a common sight throughout the summer.

– there are so many different plants

Plants for SUMMER (2)

Summer-flowering plants are more various and numerous than any others. At this time of year it is easy to create swathes of colour and dramatic beds full of contrasts.

IF YOU WANT to make a real splash of colour, fragrance and form in your garden, there is no better way to do it than by planting an eclectic mix of different summer-flowering plants. Here are some of the best and more widely available, for the entire season.

Early summer

Trees and shrubs
Abelia ×
    grandiflora
Aesculus
    hippocastanum
Buddleja globosa
    B. alternifolia
Ceanothus

Petunias, with their showy, colourful flowers, are summer perennials grown as annuals.

Cistus purpureus
Deutzia gracilis
Escallonia
Laburnum
    anagyroides,
    L. × watereri
Lonicera
    periclymenum
Malus
Philadelphus
Potentilla
Pyracantha
Rhododendron
Rosa
Spiraea douglasii
Syringa
Viburnum
    plicatum
Weigela
Wisteria sinensis

Perennials and bedding plants
Achillea
    filipendulina
    'Gold Plate'
Ageratum
Althaea
Aquilegia vulgaris
Astrantia major
Campanula
Coreopsis
Delphinium
    elatum hybrids
Dianthus
Dictamnus
    fraxinella
Digitalis purpurea
Fuchsia (bedding)
Geranium
Heuchera
Iris
Lobelia erinus
Lupinus
Nepeta × faassenii
Paeonia
Papaver orientale
Pelargonium

Bulbs
Allium
Camassia
    leichtlinii,
    C. quamash
Iris
Lilium

Midsummer

Trees and shrubs
Abelia floribunda,
    A. × grandiflora
Catalpa
    bignonioides
Ceanothus
Cistus
Clethra alnifolia
Cytisus
    battandieri
Escallonia
Eucryphia
Fuchsia
    magellanica
Genista
Helianthemum
Hibiscus
Hydrangea
    macrophylla
Hypericum
    calycinum

The delicately coloured flowers of sweet peas (these are 'Pink Expression'), add gentle beauty to any summer garden.

Lavandula
Lonicera
    periclymenum
Olearia haastii
Philadelphus
Rosa
Sparticum
    junceum
Vinca major,
    V. minor

Hemerocallis (day lily). This variety is 'Summer Trumpet'

Perennials and bedding plants
Achillea
Alstroemeria
Althaea
Astilbe × arendsii,
    A. chinensis
Astrantia major
Begonia
    semperflorens
Campanula
Chrysanthemum
    maximum
Coreopsis
Dahlia
Delphinium
    elatum hybrids
Dianthus

Digitalis purpurea
Echinops ritro
Erigeron
Fuchsia
Gaillardia ×
  grandiflora
Geranium
Geum
Gypsophila
  paniculata
Helenium
Hemerocallis
Heuchera
Hosta
Impatiens
Kniphofia
Lathyrus
Lupinus
Nepeta × faassenii
Nicotiana alata
Oenothera
Pelargonium
Penstemon
Phlox paniculata
Romneya coulteri
Scabiosa
  caucasica
Solidago

Bulbs
Allium
Cardiocrinum
  giganteum
Crocosmia ×
  crocosmiiflora
Eucomis bicolor
Gladiolus
Lilium
Tigridia pavonia

Late summer

Trees and shrubs
Abelia floribunda,
  A. × grandiflora
Buddleja davidii
Campsis radicans

Impatiens 'Blitz' (busy lizzie) is a classic summer evergreen perennial grown as an annual.

Caryopteris ×
  clandonensis
Ceanothus
Clematis
Clerodenrum
  bungei
Clethra
  alternifolia
Eucryphia
Fuchsia
Hebe
Hibiscus syriacus
Hydrangea
  macrophylla,
  H. aspera villosa

Zinnia angustifolia 'Persian Carpet' is a fast-growing, upright, bushy, annual.

Hypericum
Jasminum
  officinale
Lavandula
Leycesteria
  formosa
Lonicera
  periclymenum
Passiflora
  caerulea
Perovskia
  atriplicifolia
Rosa
Trachelospermum
  jasminoides

Perennials and bedding plants
Acanthus spinosus
Achillea
Aconitum
Alstroemeria
Althaea
Anemone japonica
Arctotis × hybrida
Aster
Astilbe × arendsii,
  A. chinensis
Begonia
  semperflorens

Campanula
Centaurea cyanus
Chrysanthemum
Echinops ritro
Felicia amelloides
Gaillardia ×
  grandiflora
Gazania
Gypsophila
  paniculata
Helenium
Helianthus
  annuus
Hemerocallis
Hosta
Impatiens
Kniphofia
Lathyrus
Nemesia fruticans
Nepeta faassenii
Nicotiana alata
Oenothera
Osteospermum
Penstemon
Phlox paniculata
Romneya coulteri
Rudbeckia
Scabiosa
  caucasica
Sedum spectabile
Zinnia
  angustifolia

Bulbs
Amaryllis
  belladonna
Crinum powellii
Crocosmia ×
  crocosmiiflora
Cyclamen
  purpurascens
Eucomis bicolor
Gladiolus hybrids,
  Gladiolus
  callianthus
Lilium

The showy blooms of Gaillardia grandiflora (blanket flower) are produced all summer. Grow the plants in a sunny well-drained site.

Cobaea scandens (cup-and-saucer vine) is a fast-growing, leafy tendril climber, usually treated as a half-hardy annual in frost-prone areas. Train it up trellis or netting.

Hydrangea aspera villosa is one of the loveliest of the lace-cap species, with broad heads of large pinkish white, sterile outer flowers surrounding small purple or blue inner ones.

Clockwise from top left:
Rudbeckia; crab apples; an
autumn garden; pumpkins;
rosehips; *Nepeta* 'Six Hills Giant'.

Autumn

PREPARATION

The last days of summer slide imperceptibly into the first days of autumn, and there is still plenty of work for the gardener to do. Leaves must be swept up before they smother lawns and plants underneath them; borders of depressed-looking perennials need to be tidied and slightly tender specimens protected against the cold, wet weather just around the corner. Fruit and vegetables must be harvested and stored safely for use in the less bountiful winter days to come.

Autumn is not just about a growing season that is drawing to an end, though – it is also a time to be getting ready for the next one. Autumn is the time for planting the bulbs that will delight us in spring. It is the main season for planting trees and shrubs, for making new lawns, for increasing border plants – and for looking ahead, and making plans to create an even better garden next year.

Autumn
AUTUMN CHECKLIST

☑ Clear away fallen leaves promptly; make leafmould.

☑ Sow new lawns from seed.

☑ Prepare the soil and plant bare-root and container-grown trees and shrubs.

☑ Stake and tie in dahlias and chrysanthemums.

☑ Plant out spring bulbs such as narcissi and crocus. Begin planting bulbs in pots for forcing.

☑ Move tender plants under cover before the first frosts.

☑ Harvest fruit and vegetables and store them as appropriate.

☑ Sow hardy annuals to overwinter outdoors for early flowers next summer.

☑ Trim evergreen hedges.

☑ Lift and divide herbaceous plants.

☑ Lift and store dahlias, gladioli and begonias when the tops have frosted.

☑ Protect slightly tender plants by mulching or by constructing shelters.

☑ Clear out summer containers and replant them for winter interest.

☑ Make new lawns from turf. Aerate, feed and topdress existing lawns; repair damage such as broken edges.

☑ Take hardwood cuttings of shrubs when the leaves have fallen.

☑ Tidy herbaceous borders; but leave dead stems on slightly tender plants to give winter protection.

Dealing with LEAVES

Deciduous trees and shrubs will lose their leaves at some time during the autumn, but it is difficult to predict exactly when this will be. Nevertheless, the gardener must be prepared to tackle this problem when it arises.

Dead leaves should be raked up from the lawn as soon after they have fallen as possible, before they rot down.

A rubber-tined rake is ideal for raking up autumn leaves, since it can be used on patios and gravel without damaging the surface.

THE DEATH OF leaves is triggered by shortening daylength; this gives deciduous plants the signal to stop producing green chlorophyll in the leaves (allowing other red and yellow pigments present to show themselves) and to start cutting off the leafstalk from the rest of the plant. Temperature has a role to play, too, particularly cold nights contrasting with warm days. Once the 'abscission layer' at the base of the leafstalk has formed, the leaf remains attached to the tree only very lightly, and will fall if shaken or disturbed. This is why an ill-timed windy spell can put paid to the display of autumn colour overnight.

When the leaves fall, they may at first be dry and crisp, but damp weather soon turns them to a slimy, brown, decaying mush. Wet, fallen leaves can smother plants underneath them, particularly low-growing and creeping plants which may be completely covered. Specimen trees often stand in the middle of lawns, which means that in autumn, dead leaves cover the grass beneath the

branches of the tree, preventing light and air reaching it and encouraging the development of fungal diseases.

Clearing up fallen leaves is a job that should be done at the first possible moment. Apart from any other considerations, the leaves are much easier and more pleasant to handle when they are still dry. Among border plants and alpines, leaves can be removed by hand or with a rubber-tined rake which will not damage the plants. The same rake can be used on lawns, but here a spring-tined rake, with flexible wire teeth, is a more popular choice. Once the leaves have been raked into heaps, they can be picked up with a pair of plastic grabs (although two pieces of wood can make a cheap and effective substitute).

There are other methods of clearing up leaves. Wheeled mechanical leaf sweepers are easy and efficient to use, sweeping the leaves into a large collecting bag, or a rotary lawnmower, with the blades set high, will whisk up fallen leaves into the grass bag. For large gardens, powered leaf blowers and garden vacuums are an option.

Rhus typhinia 'Laciniata' (stag's horn sumach) has widespreading, sparse branches with finely toothed foliage that turns orange-scarlet in autumn. If pruned regularly, it produces larger than normal foliage. It loses its leaves in early autumn.

MAKING LEAFMOULD

Deciduous leaves take a relatively long time to rot down and should not be added in large quantities to a garden compost heap for this reason. However, they are a valuable source of organic matter for the garden, and when rotted down on their own as leafmould they make an excellent soil conditioner.

Dead leaves can be packed into a container made of posts and wire netting, like a simple compost heap. Pack the leaves in layers, with a shallow covering of garden soil between every 20cm (8in) or so of leaves. Top off the heap with soil to prevent the dry leaves being blown away, and leave them until the following autumn, when they should have made a crumbly, fibrous material which is excellent for mulching or digging in to the soil.

An alternative method is to pack the leaves into a black plastic sack, again sandwiched between layers of soil. Once the sack is full, tie it firmly at the top and puncture some holes all around the sides with a garden fork to admit air. With this method the leaves usually rot down rather more quickly than they would in an open wire bin, and may be ready for use by the following spring, though a lot depends on the type of leaves used – beech and oak are usually considered best. Evergreen leaves are not suitable for making into leafmould.

Parrotia persica (Persian ironwood) is a small tree with leaves that turn rich gold and red colours in autumn. The tree has flaky grey bark which compensates visually when the leaves have been lost.

Making a NEW LAWN

Early autumn, while the soil is moist and the weather is still mild, is the ideal time to sow grass seed or to lay turf to make a new lawn.

A LAWN FROM seed needs more nurturing through its early stages than one of turf (see right), but sowing is certainly the cheapest way of making a lawn. It is also not such hard, heavy work as turfing.

The best-quality lawns are made from fine-leaved grasses such as bents and fescues, but these are difficult to look after and are not hardwearing. Most garden lawns are made from a seed mixture which contains one of the finer-leaved perennial ryegrass varieties – look for seed mixtures described as being for 'hardwearing', 'family' or 'utility' lawns.

MAKING A LAWN FROM TURF
1 Prepare and mark out the soil as if you were sowing grass seed. Dig it over, remove weeds and rake it down to a level surface and a fine crumb. Tread it lightly to firm it, and make sure it is nicely moist.
2 Lay the first row of turves just overlapping the eventual boundary if possible. Unroll or unfold

When a new turf lawn has first been laid, you can see the joins between the turves. However, these will fade in time.

Begin by digging over the area to be sown, removing all traces of perennial weeds, and rake the surface level, bringing the soil down to fine, even crumbs. If possible, leave the prepared soil for two or three weeks in order to allow the weed seeds that have been brought up to the surface to germinate. The weed seedlings can then be killed with a contact herbicide spray before sowing the grass seed. This helps the new grass to establish more easily, as it cuts down competition from the weeds.

Choose a dry, windless day for sowing. Seed should usually be sown at around 35–50g per sq m (1–1½oz per sq yd); seed suppliers may give their own recommended sowing rate for their particular mixture. Weigh out the total

each turf and lay it flat and without stretching, butting it up as closely as possible against its neighbour. Once the row is complete, tamp the turves down firmly with the flat edge of a rake, and lay a plank along the row to work from.

3 The second row of turves should be laid close up against the first, and so that the short joints between the turves in each row are staggered, like bricks in a wall.

4 In order to do this, cut the turves at each end of the row in half, using a sharp edging iron or a long-bladed knife. Turf the whole area. Finally, work a mixture of peat, sand and soil into the cracks between the turves with a broom, to help them knit together.

Most turf lawns tend to be square or rectangular in shape, not least because turves come with straight edges. If, when you have laid a basic rectangle of turf, you decide you want to soften some of the edges to allow for curved or semi-circular borders, follow the simple steps outlined below. All you will need is some sand, string, a small plastic cup, a peg, a half-moon edger and a spade.

Drive a peg into the grass and attach a length of string to it. Tie the free end of the string to a plastic cup with a hole punched in the base and fill it with sand. Pull the string taut and mark out the curve you desire by trickling the sand out of the cup.

amount of seed required for the area of lawn to be sown, then divide this quantity in half. Sow half the seed over the whole lawn working up and down, then sow the second half over the same area, working from side to side.

Once all the seed has been sown, rake it lightly into the soil surface with a spring-tined rake; it is not essential to cover the seed completely. It is often necessary to use bird scarers to deter birds from eating the seed, or cover the sown area with netting or horticultural fleece, although most lawn seed mixtures are treated with a bird repellent.

Grass seed may take up to three weeks to germinate, depending on the weather. Warm, showery conditions are ideal; if the weather remains dry,

watering may become necessary. Be sure to use a sprinkler which gives a very fine, gentle spray to avoid washing seeds or young seedlings out of the soil. When the majority of the grass seedlings have reached about 5cm (2in) high, the lawn can be cut with a mower with the blades set high, to remove just the tips of the grass blades. The mower blades must be well sharpened to cut the grass cleanly rather than tearing it, which would disturb the roots in the soil. Continue to mow the new lawn regularly, as required, gradually lowering the blades; this regular mowing will help eliminate weeds. Otherwise, avoid walking over the grass as far as possible until it has knitted together to make a firm, dense turf.

Following the sand marks, cut through the turf with a half-moon edger. Using a garden spade, remove the semi-circle of turf that you no longer want. This can be added, upside down, to the compost heap.

Autumn LAWN CARE

Like many plants, grass is subject to decay and **deterioration** in the autumn, so lawns require special care at that time.

As daylight hours shorten in the cool autumn, grass growth slows down. This means that lawn mowing gradually becomes a less frequent chore.

WARM DAYS and moist conditions in early autumn keep the grass growing fast, however, so resist the temptation to slacken off too soon: little and often is always best when it comes to mowing. The height of the mower blades should be raised now, to about 65mm (¼in) above the height of the shortest summer cut. Wormcasts often become more evident in early autumn; make sure these are scattered before mowing. It may also be necessary to brush away dew from the grass.

Feeding Autumn feeding can give the lawn a boost before winter; it is especially valuable if the lawn looks in poor condition at the end of the summer. It is essential to use the right type of fertilizer – one which is high in potash and phosphate, but low in nitrogen. Avoid spring and summer lawn fertilizers and choose one specially formulated for autumn.

Scarifying Many lawns contain a large amount of 'thatch' – a mixture of old grass clippings, dead plant material, leaf

The height of the lawnmower blades should be

litter and so on – which builds up on the lawn surface around the base of the grass plants. Thatch may prevent water penetrating the soil effectively and inhibits the growth of the grass; removing it in autumn will encourage grass plants to develop new shoots to thicken and improve the turf. Thatch can be removed by some energetic work with a spring-tined rake, but this is an exhausting job on all but small lawns.

improves the soil structure, promotes the growth of healthy grass, helps prevent thatch formation and levels out minor hollows in the lawn surface.

A mixture of sand, peat and good-quality loamy soil is used for topdressing. Six parts sand to three parts loam and one part peat is a good general purpose mix, but the proportions are variable – on heavy, badly drained soils increase the

Once the lawn has been scarified, any compacted areas should be thoroughly spiked to improve aeration to the grass roots. This will help maintain the vitality of the lawn throughout the year.

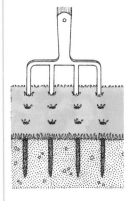

For spiking, use a garden fork, driving it deeply into the lawn and wiggling it slightly backwards and forwards before removing it and going on to make the next set of holes.

Autumn scarifying (far left) and spiking (left) are hard work, but the benefits to the lawn are enormous, and back-breaking effort in the months before winter will pay off all the year round.

An electric or petrol-driven scarifier makes the job much easier, and boxes off all the raked out material for removal.

Topdressing Topdressing involves spreading a layer of bulky organic material over the surface of the lawn and working it into the grass: this

proportion of sand, but on sandy, drought-prone soils use less sand and more peat. Estimate the amount of mixture needed by allowing roughly 1kg per sq m (3lb per sq yd) of lawn.

It is important to work the mixture down between the grass blades and not to allow it to smother the grass.

Where compaction has become a serious problem in the lawn, a tool called a hollow-tine aerator, which removes plugs of soil from the turf, can be used instead of a garden fork.

raised a little throughout the autumn

Planting TREES & SHRUBS

Autumn was always the traditional planting season for deciduous trees and shrubs. Now that the majority of plants bought are container grown, this does not apply so much, but autumn planting still has a great deal to commend it.

THE MAJOR APPEAL of container-grown plants is that they can be bought and planted at virtually any time of the year – yet, even for container-grown specimens, autumn can be the best season for planting.

Container-grown trees and shrubs have been grown in their containers all their lives. Their roots have spread throughout the compost within the pot so that, when the pot is removed, the ball of roots and compost remains intact. This means there is minimal disturbance, if any, to the roots of the tree when it is replanted.

The alternative to container-grown specimens is bare-root plants. These are grown on a field scale, and when required for sale, they are dug up from the open ground. Although various techniques are used by growers to keep root disturbance to a minimum, some damage to the roots, especially the all-important fine roots, is unavoidable. When roots are damaged, the plant's capacity to absorb water from the soil is reduced. If a tree or shrub is lifted from the open ground when it is in full leaf, the leaves will continue to lose large amounts of water through evaporation, but the damaged roots will be unable to draw enough water from the soil to replace it. This leads to the plant wilting rapidly, and being unable to establish itself in its new position.

However, once the tree or shrub is dormant, and has lost its leaves, it can be lifted from open ground and

Container-grown trees and shrubs are available for planting throughout the year, but they still do best when planted in autumn.

Once a tree or shrub is dormant, and has lost its leaves, it can be lifted from open ground and replanted without a problem

Autumn is an excellent time of year for planting trees such as this Japanese maple, to add interest to the garden.

replanted without a problem. By the time it restarts into full growth in the spring, the roots have had the opportunity to become established in the soil. There are various advantages to buying bare-root plants. They are lighter and easier to handle than container-grown specimens, so can be transported or despatched by mail order more cheaply and easily; larger

specimens can be offered for sale than is practical for container-grown subjects; and there is often more choice and variety available when plants are grown on a more extensive field scale.

The planting season extends from mid-autumn to late winter – any time the plants are dormant – but mid-autumn is probably the best time of all. The soil still retains some of its summer warmth and is unlikely to dry out as it may do in summer. The weather is usually relatively mild, and good root growth can be made before the colder winter weather sets in. Even if container-grown trees and shrubs are being planted, mid-autumn is the ideal time, allowing the plants to become properly established before the main growing season.

The ground should be prepared in advance of planting. Remember that a tree or shrub is likely to occupy the same spot for many years, so take advantage of the opportunity to improve the soil while it is available. Dig over the site thoroughly and deeply, breaking up any compacted soil layers and incorporating plenty of well-rotted compost or manure. If the soil is heavy and poorly drained, the addition of some coarse sand or grit will further improve its structure. Trees, particularly, have deep root systems, and the soil should be dug down to a depth of 60cm (24in). Remove all weeds and weed roots you may find.

There are many different shrubs and trees that will provide varied colours and interest in late autumn and on into winter.

Hamamelis mollis 'Pallida' (Chinese witch hazel) is a large upright shrub that provides good late autumn leaf colour and yellow flowers in winter.

Viburnum x *bodnantense* 'Dawn' is a hardy, large shrub with a strong upright habit. Its frost-resistant flowers appear in late autumn.

Cornus mas (cornelian cherry) is a hardy shrub with ornamental interest all year, including superbly colourful late autumn foliage.

Step-by-Step TREE PLANTING

Introducing new trees to the garden is a relatively easy way to make a strong visual impact or major change. However, new trees are surprisingly sensitive and vulnerable, and must be handled with great care.

This is a good example of a container-grown tree, with a well-established root system that has spread throughout the compost in the pot. Bare-root trees generally do not have any soil around their roots, which tend to dry out as a result.

BARE-ROOT TREES should always be planted immediately they arrive, to prevent their roots from drying out. Keep the roots covered with sacking or plastic while the tree is being transported and the planting hole is being prepared. If planting is delayed by more than a few hours, the tree should be 'heeled in' – the roots placed in a trench and covered with moist soil.

1 Dig a planting hole in the prepared ground, making it wide enough for the roots of the tree to fit comfortably when spread out, and deep enough for the tree to be at the same level at which it was growing in the nursery. On bare-root trees, the darker soil mark can be seen at the base of the trunk; with container-grown trees, the top of the rootball should be shallowly covered with soil. Pile up the soil which is removed around the hole, removing any large stones and breaking down clods.

2 Remove a container-grown tree from its pot by grasping the base of the trunk and easing out the rootball; if the compost is dry, water the container thoroughly several hours before planting. Place the rootball in the base of the planting hole and check the depth of the hole is correct – laying the wooden stake across the top of the hole is helpful. Any obviously damaged roots on a bare-root tree should be trimmed back with secateurs, and the roots spread out carefully in the base of the planting hole, with the depth being checked as before. Add or remove soil from the base of the hole as necessary to adjust the depth.

3 Once you are sure the depth is correct, add some planting mixture and slow-release fertilizer to the soil in the base of the hole. Position the tree's supporting stake at the edge of a

container-grown tree's rootball, or between the roots of a bare-root tree. Hammer the stake into place, removing the tree temporarily if it is likely to be damaged. Short stakes are the most satisfactory, since they prevent wind-rock loosening the roots while still allowing movement of the main stem, which helps the trunk to thicken up.

4 Replace the tree and begin to backfill the planting hole with soil. With containerized trees this simply involves

trickling soil down the sides of the rootball, firming it as you go. When planting bare-root trees, jiggle the tree up and down lightly as you add the first few spadesful of soil, to make sure the soil sifts down thoroughly between and beneath the roots. As you add further layers of soil, firm the tree in well by treading the soil down with the sole of your boot.

Check that you are planting the tree level and at the correct depth by laying a flat piece of wood or a bamboo cane across the hole.

Trees are versatile plants and of great ornamental value in the garden. Some offer more than one season of interest, through their foliage, flowers and bark.

Abies koreana is a slow-growing conifer of neat habit, favoured for its leaf colour and the beautiful upright, cylindrical cones it bears even when it is small.

When planting a tree, first hammer in a stout stake at the side of the hole, position the tree correctly in the hole, then backfill it. As a final step, fix the tree to the stake with a tree tie.

5 Continue until the planting hole is filled, giving a final treading over the top. Fix the tree to its stake with an adjustable tree tie, trim off any broken or damaged branches, and water the tree in thoroughly. Finally, apply a thick layer of mulch over the soil surface. The bark of newly planted trees is sometimes damaged by being eaten by deer or rabbits, or by the trunk being used by cats as a scratching post. If any of these problems seems likely to occur, place

a plastic spiral tree guard around the stem to protect it, or wrap chicken wire around it.

Recently planted trees may need watering in the spring and summer after planting, and possibly for a year or two after that. In dry spells, soak the soil around the tree thoroughly, to allow water to penetrate right through the soil to the roots. Avoid giving frequent, light waterings since this encourages roots to form in the top layer of soil, ultimately increasing the tree's susceptibility to drought.

Magnolia soulangeana 'Alexandrina' has superb, creamy flowers. Its seeds are also interesting. It needs rich soil with plenty of moisture but good drainage.

Prunus serrula is a good example of a tree grown for its shiny, coppery bark. It also sports clusters of white blossom in spring.

Dividing BORDER PLANTS

There are two reasons for dividing perennial border plants. One is to increase your stock of favourite subjects by splitting an established clump into a number of new plants, but the other is to improve the performance of the plants you have.

A border full of carefully managed perennials will brighten and enliven a garden for many years.

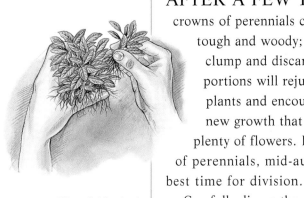

When dividing border plants, very gently split the plant into several sections with your hands, patiently teasing the sections apart without damaging them.

AFTER A FEW YEARS, the crowns of perennials can become tough and woody; splitting up the clump and discarding the older portions will rejuvenate the plants and encourage vigorous new growth that will produce plenty of flowers. For the majority of perennials, mid-autumn is the best time for division.

Carefully dig up the plant to be divided with a garden fork, keeping as much soil around the roots as possible to start with. Gently crumble or wash away some of the soil to allow you to see the crown clearly. The clump can now be split into a number of portions, each with some healthy shoots and roots.

Plants with a lot of fine, fibrous roots can often be teased into pieces just by using the fingers, but do this carefully, to keep root damage to the minimum. Dunking the roots in a bucket of water helps to get them apart without too much damage. With tougher plants, use a handfork, or two handforks back to back, to lever the portions apart. If the plant is too large or the crown too tough for this, use a pair of garden forks instead of handforks.

Some crowns are very woody indeed, and here healthy portions containing at least one, preferably two growth buds and plenty of healthy roots need to be cut away with a sharp knife. Where crowns have been cut and areas of fleshy growth have been exposed, it is a good idea to dust these cut portions with fungicide powder to prevent them rotting once the sections are replanted.

Most older perennials will have a dead, unproductive woody portion in the centre of the plant, with clusters of healthier shoots around the edge. These outside portions are the ones that

DIVIDING LARGER PLANTS
Some tough customers, such as hostas, will not respond to separation by hand or with handforks. In cases like this, use two garden forks back-to-back to lever the sections of the plant apart.

Rudbeckia fulgida 'Goldsturm' is a reliable border plant that will repay the effort involved in dividing the crowns by remaining bright and vigorous for some years.

should be retained; the woody, worn-out centre can be discarded.

It is important that the roots of plants are not allowed to dry out while they are out of the soil. Keep the roots moist by sprinkling them with water from a can fitted with a rose, and cover them over with a sack or plastic sheet while you are not actually working with them.

Once the plant is split up, replant the new portions straightaway. The new divisions are usually replanted in groups of three to replace a single, large plant, but this will depend on the space available.

If you do not have room to replant all the divisions you obtain, the surplus pieces can be potted up and left in a sheltered place outside in the garden over winter. Check that the soil remains moist. They may be useful to replace any winter losses when next spring comes around.

Herbaceous perennials will thrive for years and are the mainstay of a successful border. These are some of the best.

Aconitum napellus (monk's hood) has deep blue hooded flowers. Cut down the flowered stems and divide the roots in autumn.

Solidago (golden rod) will soon exhaust the soil if it is not regularly divided and replanted during autumn and winter.

Cut back the vigorous *Nepeta* x *faassinii* 'Six Hills Giant' (catmint) in autumn. Divide it later in the winter, when the soil warms up.

Overwintering PLANTS

Most gardens contain a number of tender plants that will not survive the winter out of doors. Some are difficult or expensive to replace, and need special care to keep them alive over winter.

Overwinter the roots of florists' spray chrysanthemums and all dahlias under cover.

Dahlia 'Fascination' is a late-flowering dwarf dahlia which flowers from summer through into autumn.

THE DEFINITION of 'tender' is not exact (see page 130), and there are several plants that will grow very happily in a reasonably sheltered place outdoors in temperate climates during the summer, but will begin to struggle in the cooler days of early autumn and be killed by the first touch of frost.

There are several ways of keeping these plants going during the winter. Which is the most appropriate depends on the plant's type and size, and the facilities available.

Moving under cover If suitable space is available and the plant is a practical size, the whole plant can be moved to a frost-free greenhouse or conservatory in early autumn, before the first frost is likely. This is a good way to treat containerized shrubs and small trees, or plants that it has taken several years to train into attractive shapes, such as standard fuchsias or marguerites. Moving these plants is made easier if the pots are permanently positioned on wooden plant stands fitted with castors.

Move tender plants into the greenhouse in

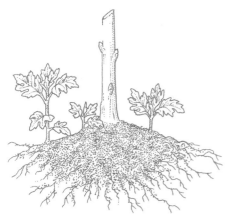

OVERWINTERED CHRYSANTHEMUMS
In spring, the overwintered stools of chrysanthemums will produce new shoots which are ideal for use as softwood cuttings.

Preserving the roots Several plants produce a rootstock which is rather hardier than the topgrowth, and will remain dormant but alive in a cool place over winter. When spring comes, it can be started into growth and can either be planted out at the appropriate time, or the new shoots can be used as cuttings. The rootstock is often fleshy, such as the rhizomes of cannas, the tubers of begonias, or the tuberous roots of dahlias. Once the topgrowth has been blackened by frost, the roots can be lifted, cleaned off, and stored in very slightly moist peat or similar material for the winter. A frost-free shed or garage is a suitable place.

Insurance from cuttings Sometimes it is not possible or necessary to keep the original plant for the following year. Softwood stem cuttings can often be rooted during the summer months and overwintered in small pots in a frost-free greenhouse, ready for planting out after the risk of frosts is over the following spring or early summer. It is a good idea to take a few cuttings as an insurance policy from 'dubiously hardy' plants which normally come through the winter unscathed outdoors. Should the parent plant be killed by an unexpectedly cold spell, at least there will be replacements available.

Tuberous-rooted border dahlias are a good example of plants that need to be lifted and overwintered in dry, frost-free conditions until late spring or early summer.

Lift dahlia tubers with a fork when their foliage dies back in autumn. Trim their stems down to about 15cm (6in), and turn them upside down to dry.

Carefully wrap each plant in several sheets of newspaper, leaving the top end of each newspaper packet open to the air.

Place each wrapped plant in a paper bag, again leaving the top of the bag open. Stand the bags in a box and store them in a cool, dry, frost-free place over winter.

early autumn, before the first frost

Preparing SPRING BULBS

Not all spring-flowering bulbous plants grow from a bulb; several, such as Anemone blanda, are root tubers. This low-growing little plant bears pale blue, mauve, pink and white flowers in early spring. It will thrive in a rock garden or in any well-drained soil.

THE FLOWERING of spring bulbs is one of the most eagerly anticipated spectacles of the gardener's calendar, and autumn is the time to start making it happen. Keep a look-out for bulbs appearing in the shops from early autumn onwards – the best quality and best choice of varieties will be available early in the season.

Some of the favourite spring-flowering plants are true bulbs, while others are in fact corms and tubers, but for convenience they are all referred to simply as bulbs. They are the dormant storage organs of the plant, and already contain the flower buds for the following season within them. This means that the quality of the bulbs you buy is all-important; no matter how well you grow them, they cannot produce flowers if the buds are not already present at planting time.

Look for large bulbs; ones that are small for their type are less likely to flower well. The bulbs should be plump and firm, with a well-developed growing point; if there is a scaly outer protective coat it should be intact, and there must be no sign of disease or damage visible. Reject bulbs that look shrivelled, are soft, or have already sprouted shoots.

Daffodils, jonquils, narcissi and tulips are all well-known true bulbs. Bulbs consist of fleshy leaves wrapped around an embryo flower bud, and around the outside there is usually a dry, papery protective skin.

which are prone to damage by cold weather. If for any reason bulbs cannot be planted shortly after they are obtained, they should be stored in a cool, dark place, preferably spaced out

Bulbs should always be plump and firm, with a well-developed growing point

Gladioli and crocus grow from corms – swollen stem bases with a bud at the top. Daughter corms develop from small buds that form at the base of the parent.

Once the bulbs have been obtained, they should usually be planted as soon as possible. This prevents them continuing to lose moisture to the air and gives them a long growing season to make good root growth. Some bulbs, however, such as tulips and hyacinths, should not be planted before mid- to late autumn. If they are planted too early, they produce premature leafy shoots

in a seed tray so that they are not touching each other. A covering of soil-less potting compost will help to prevent them from shrivelling if the planting delay is extended. Use the compost as it comes from a fresh bag – do not add any water.

Different bulbs have slightly different growing requirements, but most prefer a light, free-draining soil, since they are prone to rotting if planted in badly drained soil where moisture lies around them. Heavy soils can be improved by incorporating some coarse sand, and all soils will benefit from the addition of well-rotted organic matter such as garden compost or manure. This should be dug into the site before the bulbs are obtained. Fertilizer is not necessary before planting.

Eranthis hyemalis (winter aconite) is an early-flowering tuberous plant, with cup-shaped flowers surrounded by ruffs of bracts in very early spring.

Arum italicum 'Pictum' (lords and ladies) produces ornamental leaves in mid-spring and bright red berries in autumn.

Galanthus 'S. Arnott' (snowdrop) is an early-flowering bulb which has larger flowers than most species of snowdrop.

Planting Spring BULBS

It is easy to get carried away when buying bulbs, visualizing only the magnificent display their flowers will make in the spring, and forgetting the hard work of planting them all.

A lawn full of brightly coloured crocuses is a delight, but planting them all in the first place can be hard work.

The ideal tool for planting bulbs is a special device with a cylindrical blade beneath the handle which removes a plug of soil when pushed into the ground.

THE CORRECT TOOLS are

vital – a good, strong-necked, wide-bladed trowel with a comfortable handle, or a special bulb-planting device which removes a core of soil.

The planting site for bulbs should, wherever possible, be dug over deeply before planting as this makes it much easier to set bulbs at the correct depth.

Planting patterns Bulbs are nearly always best when planted in informal groups. The usual technique is to scatter them randomly over the area. Trying to space them out equally nearly always looks forced and planting in straight rows should be avoided at all costs.

PLANTING BULBS IN GRASS (1)
Planting bulbs in grass can be very hard work. Water the turf thoroughly for several days before planting in order to soften it. Space the bulbs out randomly where you intend to plant them.

PLANTING DEPTHS FOR BULBS
This table shows the ideal depth of planting for a variety of different common bulb types. The scale shows centimetres on the left and inches on the right. 1 *Lilium candidum*; 2 *Cyclamen persicum*; 3 *Pushkinia*; 4 *Acidanthera bicolor*; 5 *Scilla siberica*; 6 *Galanthus nivalis*; 7 *Iris reticulata*; 8 *Narcissus* 'Trevithian'; 9 *Muscari*; 10 *Lilium auratum*; 11 *Fritillaria imperialis*.

Planting depth This depends on the size of the bulb. As a general rule, the depth of soil above the nose of the bulb should be at least twice the height of the bulb itself – which means the base of the planting hole must be three times the height of the bulb.

PLANTING BULBS IN GRASS (2)
Where possible, dig the individual holes with a trowel, but if the grass is too tough, use a long-handled, foot-operated planting tool. Alternatively, cut the turf with a spade to expose the soil.

Planting techniques Bulbs can be planted individually or as a group. When planting individually, dig a straight-sided hole to the correct depth, making sure it is wide enough to accept the bulb. Be careful that the hole does not become narrower towards the base, or the bulb may become lodged partway down so that its base is not in contact with the soil. Prick over the base of the hole and place the bulb in it firmly, giving it a little twist to settle it into the soil. Refill the hole with soil and firm lightly.

It is sometimes easier to dig one large hole for a group of bulbs. Dig it out to the correct depth, scatter the bulbs in the base and then set them in position with their noses upright. It is a good idea to label patches of bulbs as they are planted, otherwise it can be very easy to forget where they are and dig them up accidentally.

Spring-flowering bulbs are rewarding plants. If given a general liquid fertilizer after flowering, many will continue to bloom for years.

The unusual *Fritillaria meleagris* (snake's head fritillary), with its chequered petals, grows well in short grass in damp conditions.

Muscari armeniacum, (grape hyacinth) produces dense flowers and will spread by self-sown seeds and bulbils if undisturbed.

Ideal for moist shade, *Erythronium tuolumnense* 'Pagoda' bears sulphur-yellow flowers on stems up to 40cm (18in) long.

Bulbs for THE HOME

One way of shortening the winter a little is to grow early-flowering spring bulbs in the home.

FOR MOST gardeners, spring cannot come soon enough. Growing a few early-flowering bulbs indoors gives a splendid foretaste of the colour and fragrance that is still a few weeks away in the open garden.

Most bulbs require a low-temperature trigger to begin the flowering process; flowers will not develop until the temperature has been below 9°C (48°F) for a number of weeks (the length of time varies according to the type of bulb). During this cool period, a strong root system is

PLANTING BULBS IN CONTAINERS
It is important to get an even, well-spread growing pattern in your bowl or pot once your bulbs flower. Ensure this is the case by spacing the bulbs evenly in the soil, in smooth circles and patterns.

formed. Bulbs can be 'forced' into flower earlier than their natural season by keeping them in cool temperatures for the required number of weeks, then bringing them into the warmth to encourage flower buds to open.

Plant the bulbs in early to mid-autumn in pots or decorative bowls. Always choose a container with

Hyacinths are probably the most popular bulbs for forcing – at least in Europe. For extra-early flowers, buy specially prepared, or 'treated' bulbs.

The Parrot tulip *Tulipa* 'Orange Favourite' has large blooms, with typically twisted and irregularly fringed petals.

One particular type of *Narcissus* – the Tazetta hybrids – can be grown without bothering with a cold, dark period. 'Paper White' is the most popular variety.

deep enough to completely cover the pots. A shed, garage or basement is also suitable, as long as the temperature can be kept fairly even and between 1–13°C (33–55°F). Make a note of the date the bulbs were planted and when they will need to be removed, and check them occasionally in the interim to ensure that the compost remains moist.

Once the required number of weeks is up, move the bulbs into full light, but continue to keep them in a cool position. The flower buds should be well developed before the bowls are moved into a warmer room (about 19°C/65°F) to bring them into full flower and fragrance.

A low-growing tulip, *Tulipa clusiana* var. *chrysantha* bears long yellow flowers. There are often two flowers to a stem.

drainage holes – it makes caring for the bulbs easier. Place some 5cm (2in) or more of soilless potting compost in the base of the container and sit the bulbs on top of it, so that their noses are just below the level of the rim. Set the bulbs closely together – just touching – for the best results, but keep to one variety per pot to make sure they all flower together. Fill in around them with more compost until the container is full, then water gently with a fine rose on the can until the compost is just moist.

The planted container must then be placed somewhere cool and completely dark for the required number of weeks. In cold areas this can be in the garden, either at the base of a trench in the ground or in a 'plunge bed' of sand or ashes that is

Narcissi and hyacinths are the most popular bulbs for forcing, but other bulbs less commonly grown can be just as successful.

Bulb and weeks of cold treatment:
Chionodoxa luciliae 15
Crocus chrysanthus, C. vernus 15
Eranthis hyemalis 15
Fritillaria meleagris 15
Galanthus nivalis 15
Hyacinthus (prepared) 10–12
Hyacinthus (not prepared) 11–14
Iris danfordiae, I. reticulata 15
Muscari armeniacum 13–15
Narcissus 15–17
Scilla siberica 15
Tulipa 10–20

Tulipa 'Angelique' is a scented, double, late-blooming peony-flowered tulip. Its pale pink flowers are striped with lighter pink.

Bulbs for THE HOME **125**

Sowing for SUMMER COLOU[R]

For early summer flowers in the garden next year, many hardy annuals can be sown outdoors in autumn. In most areas, seedlings will stand over the winter and have a head start over spring-sown plants.

SOW THE SEEDS where they are to flower, in just the same way as for spring sowings (see page 18). Choose the most sheltered site available and, in early autumn, sow the seeds thinly in short drills, covering them lightly with soil; watering is not normally necessary at this time of year. Given warm, moist weather, seeds should germinate quickly, and the seedlings can be given a preliminary thinning as soon as they are large enough. Do not thin them to their final spacings yet, though – leave that until spring, to allow for a number of losses over winter. Ensure that you keep the seedlings weed free.

Sow seeds of the tall *Digitalis purpurea* (foxglove) – a perennial, grown as a biennial – in autumn.

and summer. If you didn't get round to sowing your own seed, young plants can usually be obtained from garden centres and shops now.

Biennials are plants that take two years to complete their life cycle, growing from seed in one year and flowering in the next. True biennials die after flowering, but some plants, which are in fact perennials and would continue to grow for several years, are treated by gardeners as biennials because they deteriorate after their first flowering season and are not worth keeping.

Biennials are usually planted once the summer bedding has been cleared away. Dig the soil over thoroughly, removing all weeds, and work in an application of fertilizer or bonemeal.

The spacing of the plants will depend on their size, and varies from 15–30cm (6–12in). Plant with a trowel,

The annual Dwarf Mixed *Coreopsis tinctoria* (tickseed) flowers freely in sunny, well-drained soil, in shades of yellow and rust.

Planting biennials If you raised some biennials from seed earlier in the year, mid-autumn is the time to plant them out where they are to flower in spring

aking care to firm well, and water the plants in immediately after planting. Further watering may be needed if there is a dry spell in the following weeks. Young plants bought from a garden shop should be planted out as soon as possible after purchase.

Spring-flowering biennials, such as forget-me-nots and wallflowers, are often planted along with bulbs like

The saucer-shaped flowers of Californian poppy, with lustrous petals, light up the garden in summer.

tulips and hyacinths to give an attractive display – stately white or pink tulip flowers floating gracefully over a blue haze of forget-me-nots make a superb sight in late spring. Check the height of the varieties chosen and adjust planting positions to make sure that taller-growing biennials will not stand in front of, and obscure, the flowers of the bulbs.

Not all hardy annuals do well from an autumn sowing. Those that often give good results include:

Calendula (pot marigold)
Centaurea cyanus (cornflower)
Centaurea moschata (sweet sultan)
Clarkia amoena (godetia)
Consolida ambigua (larkspur)
Coreopsis tinctoria (tickseed)
Echium vulgare (viper's bugloss)
Eschscholzia californica
    (Californian poppy)
Gypsophila elegans (baby's breath)
Iberis amara (candytuft)
Lavatera trimestris (mallow)
Limnanthes douglasii
    (poached egg plant)
Lobularia maritima (sweet alyssum)
Nigella damascena (love-in-a-mist)
Papaver rhoeas (shirley poppy)
Scabiosa atropurpurea (sweet
    scabious, pincushion flower)
Silene coeli-rosea
    (viscaria, rose of heaven)

Popular biennials include:

Bellis perennis (double daisy)
Campanula medium
    (Canterbury bell)
Erysimum cheiri (wallflower)
Dianthus barbatus
    (sweet william)
Digitalis purpurea (foxglove)
Lunaria annua (honesty)
Myosotis (forget-me-not)
Matthiola incana (Brompton stock)

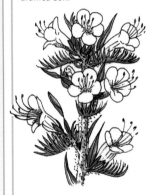

Papaver rhoeas (shirley poppy) is a fully hardy annual grown for its cup-shaped flowers. It requires sun or semi-shade and prefers moist but well-drained soil.

Echium vulgare (viper's bugloss) is good for autumn sowing, providing beautiful flowers throughout the spring. Whitefly can be troublesome to these plants.

Calendula (pot marigold) is a reliable spring annual that does well when sown in autumn. Deadhead the plants to prolong flowering.

Containers for WINbsp TER

Containers need not be stored away after the popular summer flowering season – they can be planted up to give plenty of interest over the winter, too.

PLANTS IN containers are prone to damage by cold conditions. Their roots are above ground, so they do not have the protection of the soil – just a small amount of compost to insulate them. Lining the inside of the containers with insulating material such as bubble polythene (punctured to allow drainage) is worthwhile in cold areas, and they should be placed in sheltered positions over the winter.

Winter plantings need not be dull. Here, the creamy white ornamental kale dominates, with bright skimmia berries. The central brachyglottis gives height and structure, and ivy softens the outline.

PLANTING CONTAINERS FOR WINTER
When summer-flowering containers start to look jaded in early to mid-autumn, clear out the plants and soil. Refill with fresh potting compost and plant up subjects for winter interest, such as those shown here: *Erica carnea* 'Springwood White', *Vinca minor* f. *alba* and *Euonymus fortunei* 'Harlequin'.

While there are plenty of winter-flowering plants, some of the main winter interest comes from form and foliage, rather than blooms. Evergreens play a very important role; the variegated types, particularly, provide some bright winter colour. Winter- and early spring-flowering bulbs are invaluable and there are many smaller varieties – providing colour and often scent – which are suitable for window boxes and other small containers.

As with summer containers, plant to provide a pleasing contrast and combination of heights, forms and colours. Dwarf conifers and shrubs provide a little height, while trailers, such as ivy, cascade attractively, softening harsh edges.

Autumn

In larger containers, some of the evergreens can be permanent residents, with summer-flowering plants being set around them in season. It is best to grow the evergreens in their own pots, sunk in the compost within the container – this helps control their size and makes replanting the containers easier. In smaller containers, most of the plants will probably be used as winter bedding, being removed in spring and either discarded or replanted in the open to grow on. Garden centres sell a wide range of ready-potted plants.

Ornamental cabbage or kale, *Brassica oleracea*, are highly ornamental forms, with large crinkled leaves in attractively mixed shades.

Suitable plants There are interesting subjects to choose from. The following suggestions will give a good show of colour and form, but try experimenting with others, too.

Ajuga reptans 'Atropurpurea', *A. r.* 'Multicolor'(bugle)
Anemone blanda
Brassica oleracea forms (ornamental cabbage)
Buxus sempervirens 'Suffruticosa', *B. microphylla* 'Compacta', *B. m.* 'Green Pillow'(box)
Calluna vulgaris 'Golden Feather', *C. v.* 'Sir John Charrington', *C. v.* 'Spring Cream'(heather, ling)

Chionodoxa luciliae (glory of the snow)
Crocus chrysanthus
Cyclamen coum
Juniperus communis 'Compressa'
Eranthis hyemalis (winter aconite)
Erica carnea, many varieties (winter-flowering heath)
Euonymus fortunei 'Harlequin', *E. f.* 'Silver Queen'
Galanthus nivalis (snowdrop)

Hebe albicans, *H. pinguifolia* 'Pagei'
Hedera helix many varieties (ivy)
Helleborus niger (Christmas rose)
Narcissus 'February Gold', *N.* 'February Silver'
Thymus citriodorus 'Golden King', *T. vulgaris* 'Silver Posie' and others (thyme)
Viola x *wittrockiana* Universal Series (winter-flowering pansies)

Cyclamen coum, the winter-flowering cyclamen, with silver-patterned leaves, bears a succession of pink flowers throughout the season.

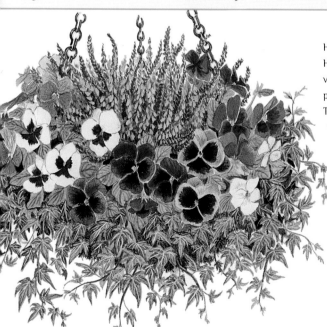

HANGING BASKETS
Hanging baskets are particularly vulnerable to frost and generally poor weather conditions in winter. This is because of their very small volume of soil and all-round exposure, but in a sheltered corner they are worth trying in milder climates. Select plants such as winter-flowering pansy, winter-flowering heath and an ivy like 'Green Ripple'. Some of the plants suggested above are suitable.

The cup-shaped yellow flowers of perennial *Eranthis hyemalis* (winter aconite) are stemless and arise directly from a knobbly tuber.

Preparing for WINGTER

As winter approaches, some plants require protection or need to be moved indoors, except in regions that enjoy mild winter weather.

Extreme weather conditions require extreme forms of protection for plants.

PLANTS ARE OFTEN

classified into two main groups – hardy and tender – but there are no hard and fast definitions for these terms. 'Hardy' is usually taken to mean that a plant is able to spend the whole year out of doors without needing any special protection against cold weather. What this really means will vary according to the region in which you live, and how cold local winters are, but it generally means that plants will withstand some degree of frost without damage. Tender plants, on the other hand, will definitely not withstand frost, and may require minimum temperatures several degrees above freezing. To add to the confusion, terms such as 'dubiously hardy' and 'slightly tender' are used as well. These often describe plants which may overwinter outside quite happily for a number of years, only to succumb to a slightly colder-than-normal spell in a subsequent winter season.

Which plants need winter protection and which do not will vary not only from country to country and region to region, but also from one garden to another within a neighbourhood – local conditions can be completely different within a very small area. Most gardeners learn from often rather bitter experience just what they can get away with in their own gardens.

Providing protection against cold

Plants that are likely to need some form of cold protection are those often labelled 'dubiously hardy'. Sometimes the topgrowth of such plants dies back in autumn, and it is the rootstock that requires extra help through the winter. This can be provided by mulching the top of the soil over the root area in mid- to late autumn with a heavy application of an insulating material such as peat. Dry, dead leaves, loose straw or dead bracken can also be used.

Where there is topgrowth above ground that needs protecting, construct a framework around the plant with stakes and wire netting, packing this loosely with straw, bracken or dry leaves as before. Don't fill it tightly – it is important to maintain some air movement around the plant.

Trees, shrubs and climbers that are susceptible to cold weather are often grown against a sheltered wall; this is a popular way to grow rather tender fruits such as peaches and apricots. The easiest way to protect these against cold weather is to construct a 'roller blind' of netting. Fix a length of wood to the wall above the plant to be protected, extending to the full width of the plant.

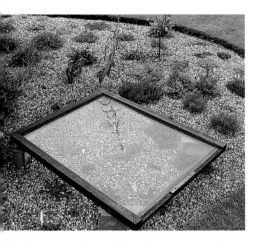

Provide protection from rain for alpines by laying a sheet of glass, raised on wood or bricks, over them.

each end and roll it up like a roller blind, securing it in place with ties. Fix the roll to the length of wood attached to the wall, ensuring that it is the correct way up, so the netting can be untied and unrolled over the plant to be protected in extreme weather.

The most vulnerable time for fruit trees is in very early spring when they start to flower, but the structure should be in place by autumn so that it is ready for use when needed. Cold weather and frosts during the dormant season are not as damaging as those that arrive in late winter and early spring, once growth has started. Take care not to remove protection too early from vulnerable plants, or tender new shoots may be killed.

Obtain a piece or pieces of netting or fleece of a suitable width to fit this piece of wood, and long enough to reach nearly to the ground. Tack the netting or fleece to a lathe of wood at

Plants and trees from warmer climates require particular attention during winter. *Eucalyptus* spp. originated in the southern hemisphere and many will not comfortably withstand the cold without protection. *E. gunnii* (below) is hardy.

Plants that may need protection in all but mild, sheltered gardens:
Agapanthus
Aloysia triphylla
Campsis radicans
Carpenteria californica
Clianthus puniceus
Desfontainia spinosa
Eccremocarpus scaber
Escallonia
Eucalyptus (some)
Eucomis
Eucryphia
Fremontodendron californicum
Fuchsia
Leptospermum scoparium
Melianthus major
Myrtus communis
Passiflora caerulea

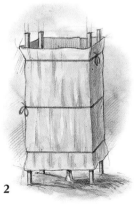

1   2   3

WINTER PROTECTION FOR PLANTS

1 A large tender shrub can be protected by covering it in horticultural fleece and tying rope firmly around the bush. Mulch around the base of the plant for additional protection.

2 To protect a young tree during winter, place stakes in a square around it and then wrap hessian or plastic sheeting around the stakes. Use garden twine to tie the sheeting securely around the square of stakes.

3 Straw packed around a wigwam of canes makes good protection for half-hardy plants such as yucca.

Autumn Care of PONDS

Autumn is the time to check over a garden pond and prepare it for winter; essential jobs must be done if the pond is to remain healthy and trouble free the following year.

Ponds can become badly congested, overgrown and dirty by autumn, when they need careful attention.

OXYGENATING PLANTS

are vital to keep the water in good condition, but they are often extremely vigorous and produce far more growth than is wanted. Early autumn is the time of year to cut them back hard, thinning out the growth by up to half, and removing all the cut-off pieces from the water. At the same time, remove as many as possible of the old, dead and dying leaves and flowers of water lilies and other water plants. If left, rotting vegetation of any kind causes a build-up of toxic gases in the pool.

If the pond contains tender plants, such as water hyacinth and water lettuce, these must be removed before the first frosts. They can be overwintered under cover in a container of water ready to put back into the pond next spring. Even if you don't intend to keep the plants for another year, remove them from the pond – once the frost has killed them they will only pollute the water as they rot.

Just before autumn leaves begin to fall from the trees, net the pond to keep the leaves out of the water. Use a fine

Artificial herons sited at the edge of the pond are said to keep real ones away, but this is often not very effective.

Remove tender plants from the pond before the first frosts and keep them in water in a sheltered place during the winter.

mesh net and support it on stakes so that it is clear of the water surface.

Continue to remove decaying vegetation from marginal and water plants throughout the autumn, using a net to scoop up debris in the centre of the pond if it is difficult to reach.

As long as the weather is mild and fish are still active, continue to feed them in early autumn to build them up for winter.

If herons visit your pond and steal fish (not an uncommon occurrence in some

areas) the problem can increase in autumn, when floating leaves die down and make the fish more visible. Leaving the pond netted over throughout the winter is probably the only way to prevent this, although a 'tripwire' of twine supported on stakes round the pond margin may help by preventing herons wading into the water.

Finally, submersible pumps which have been running fountains and waterfalls should now be removed, cleaned and overhauled, and stored away for the winter.

A successful pond depends on plants. Many serve a practical purpose. Oxygenators, which are often totally submerged, help to keep the water clear and provide oxygen and shelter for fish. Floating plants and deep-water ones with floating leaves cut down the amount of sunlight on the water surface, so helping to control the growth of algae. They also provide shelter for wildlife, as do the flowering marginals, such as rushes and iris.

Most water plants die back in winter, and their top-growth must be removed. When you take out a clump of decaying weed, leave it by the pond for a while so that any creatures in it can return to the water.

CUTTING BACK MARGINALS
When the leaves and stems of marginal plants have turned brown, cut them down to about 7–10cm (3–4in) above the water line. This will help to keep the plants healthy and will also remove any foliage pests infesting them.

BIODEGRADABLE STRAW PADS
These are excellent for controlling algae in ponds year-round. Consisting of barley straw and a natural cotton netting overcoat, the pads float on the surface of the pond, keeping down algae and preventing the water from freezing over in winter.

Other plants, such as *Eichhornia crassipes* (water hyacinth) with spikes of pale mauve flowers in summer, are tender, but will survive if overwintered in water in a frost-free place.

Autumn WILDLIFE

Many wild creatures are useful in the garden and should be encouraged and protected as much as possible. Autumn is a time when they need particular care.

SOME CREATURES may not be particularly useful but are welcome all the same, simply because they are decorative and interesting. Winter is hard for nearly all forms of wildlife, when food and water may be scarce and the weather inhospitable. Autumn is a good time to supply food to build up their reserves for the tough season ahead, and to provide shelters or hibernation sites for those creatures that might make use of them.

Providing food Growing plants which produce berries and seeds will provide a food source for a wide range of creatures, although birds are the most noticeable visitors that will take advantage of the harvest. However, small mammals such as mice and voles will also take their share of seeds and fruits, especially those that have been dropped by the birds.

Insects also need to take advantage of autumn food sources. Butterflies, especially Red Admirals, can often be seen feeding on rotting apples, and a flowering ivy plant will be thronged with insect life making the most of its late nectar

No one will object to sharing the autumn plenty of the garden with a creature as endearing as this little wood mouse.

Hedgehogs must build up fat stores before hibernating.

supply. Ivy needs to reach the top of its climb to produce flowers: these form on arborescent shoots which are quite different to the climbing stems. Train a plant over a low wall or tree stump, or

One of the best ways to provide shelter for

Many garden fruits are beneficial to wildlife during the autumn and winter. As well as birds, small mammals will thrive on a variety of autumnal seeds and berries.

Elderberries are ubiquitous wild garden fruits beloved of blackbirds, thrushes and other common birds.

left-over breakfast cereals and so on are all useful. Wholemeal bread is more valuable than white; all bread is best moistened with water before it is put out.

Another garden visitor who sometimes appreciates a meal provided for him is the hedgehog – an extremely valuable predator of slugs and snails, and well worth encouraging. Do not be tempted to put out bread and milk, as is often advised – milk causes often fatal digestive problems. Tinned cat food is fine.

Providing shelter One of the best ways to provide shelter for wildlife is to do nothing – to leave a section of the garden wild and overgrown. Add some logs, a wooden box or two, a section of pipe, a paving slab propped up slightly at one side, and a piece of corrugated iron laid on soft earth. An old shed, preferably with loose roof tiles and gaps in the woodwork, is also very valuable. Bats, reptiles and amphibians, insects and small mammals – in fact, a wide range of creatures of all types – will be able to find homes for the winter in such an area.

Hedgehogs can be encouraged to remain in the garden by providing a box in which they can hibernate over winter. Have such a box in place by early autumn.

Rosa moyesii 'Geranium' (species rose) produces lovely flagon-shaped hips during autumn.

Sunflower seeds are a tasty and rich source of nutrition for many different birds and small mammals.

grow an ivy bush from a cutting taken from an arborescent shoot.

As the autumn weather turns colder, supplement natural foods with bought-in nuts and seeds, and scraps from the house. Overripe fruit, cake and bread crumbs (especially wholemeal bread),

wildlife is to do absolutely nothing

Harvesting FRUIT

Wrap sound apples carefully in paper and store them in slatted wooden boxes; set aside and cook damaged fruit as soon as possible.

Most soft fruit is harvested during the summer, but many tree fruits, and some varieties of soft fruit, are ready to pick in early to mid-autumn.

SOME FRUITS are at their best eaten fresh, but other types can often be stored away for use through the winter months.

Apples Early apples can be picked in late summer, but the majority of varieties are not ready until early to mid-autumn. Some varieties ripen to a golden yellow or have red-flushed skin, but others remain green and it is difficult to tell from their appearance whether they are ripe or not. An apple should be lifted carefully; if the stalk separates easily from the spur, it is ready for picking.

Apples which are to be stored must be handled gently at harvest time. Lift them from the tree in the palm of the hand – do not put pressure on the skin of the fruit with the finger tips, since this could damage the fruit.

Pears Pears are a little more difficult to deal with than apples as they need to be picked just before they are ripe. Once they are fully ripe, they must be eaten within a day or two or the flesh will turn unpleasantly soft and 'sleepy'. Pick the fully formed fruits while they are still hard. Different varieties are ready from early to late autumn.

Some fruits can be stored away for use during the winter months

Plums Plums start ripening from mid-summer, but several varieties, including 'Edward's', 'Kirke's Blue', 'Marjorie's Seedling' and 'Cambridge Gage', produce their crop in early to mid-autumn. When plums are ready for picking their flesh is just soft; the skins may be golden, flecked with brown, or deep purple rather than red or pink. The stalks should separate readily from the spurs.

Cut off bunches of ripe grapes with secateurs; they will keep in a cool, dark place for several weeks.

Strawberries While most strawberries produce their crop in midsummer, there are a number of autumn-fruiting or perpetual varieties, such as 'Calypso' and 'Aromel', that produce ripe fruit in early autumn.

Raspberries Like strawberries, most raspberries are ready for harvest in midsummer, but autumn-fruiting varieties produce fruit on the current year's canes rather than last season's.

Blackberries Early autumn is the traditional time for wild blackberry picking, and although some of the garden varieties ripen earlier, this is still the main harvest season. Fruits should be plump and glossy, and fully black, not red. Most varieties separate freely from the plug when ripe.

Blueberries Blueberries ripen over some three to four weeks. The earliest varieties begin cropping in late summer, but many extend into early or mid-autumn.

Grapes The time when grapes are ready for picking varies according to the climate, variety and weather, but the season may extend from early to late autumn.

Pears such as 'William's Bon Chrétien' must be picked just before they are ripe and eaten within a few days, or the flesh becomes soft and 'sleepy'.

Countless different varieties of eating apples are grown; this is 'Starking'. It has sweet yellow flesh and keeps well. Apples bruise easily, so pick them carefully.

Cooking apples, such as 'Bramley's Seedling', taste sour and are not good for eating raw, but have many culinary uses. They keep for about four months.

Storing FRUIT

Fruit is available fresh from the garden during the summer and early autumn months, but it can be enjoyed all the year round if it is stored correctly.

Check stored apples frequently, especially when they are not wrapped, and remove any rotten ones.

Pears can be stored over winter, but they require careful handling. Wrapping pears in paper may help to check the spread of rot, but they need to be inspected frequently.

STORAGE METHODS range from the very simple to the more complex, but all are within the range of home gardeners.

Cold store Many varieties of apples and pears can be stored for several weeks or even months in a cool, dark, airy place.

Apples with a waxy skin tend to store best; russetted varieties also usually keep well. Among the best-keeping dessert varieties are 'Ashmead's Kernel', 'Brownlees Russet', 'Fiesta', 'Jonagold' and 'May Queen': good cookers are 'Arthur Turner', 'Bramley's Seedling' and 'Royal Russet'. Fewer pears keep well, but 'Doyenné du Comice', 'Glou Morceau', 'Joséphine de Malines' and 'Winter Nelis' can be stored for several weeks.

Fruit for storing must be completely unblemished and handled very carefully to avoid bruising. Individual fruits should be wrapped in a sheet of greaseproof paper, tissue or newspaper and placed carefully in wooden, slatted boxes.

Stack the boxes of fruit in a cool, dark place; a cellar is ideal, but garages or sheds can also be used. A slightly moist atmosphere delays shrivelling, but good ventilation is essential. Inspect the fruit regularly, immediately removing any showing signs of rotting.

Freezing Freezing is an excellent way of preserving the flavour of fruit, although it tends to spoil the texture. Raspberries, blackberries, gooseberries and all types of currants can be prepared as for eating fresh, and open-frozen on trays. Many fruits, particularly plums and cherries, store well when packed into freezer

Ripe autumn fruit epitomizes the plenty of the season. Why not share the abundance by giving a basketful to friends and relatives?

containers and covered with sugar syrup made from 400–600g sugar per litre of water (8–12oz per pint). Grapes can also be successfully frozen, either unsweetened or in a sugar syrup. Freeze seedless grapes whole, but skin and remove the pips from seeded varieties.

Preserves Jam making is a traditional and successful way of storing all kinds of fruit. Fruits high in pectin – such as

cooking apples, currants, gooseberries – make the best-setting jam; fruits low in pectin, such as strawberries and cherries, can be mixed with high-pectin types for a better result.

Bottling Special jars and lids are available in which to bottle and vacuum pack fruit. Prepare the fruit as for eating, pack it into the clean jars and cover with sugar syrup. Heat the filled jars to sterilize the contents, and at the end of the recommended heating time, tighten the lids to ensure a vacuum seal.

Drying Apples, pears and plums can all be dried. Peel and slice apples and pears and dip in salted water to prevent browning; halve and stone plums. Spread on racks and place in an oven at 50°C (120°F) for 6 hours. Store in ventilated jars and soak before using.

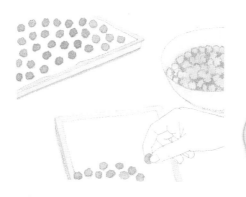

FREEZING RASPBERRIES
Rapsberries are a good fruit for freezing, since their texture remains largely unaffected. Place the raspberries on trays, leaving space around each one so that the fruits do not freeze together; when frozen, store them in bags or containers.

Lush, tasty figs can be grown in the garden in milder climates or in a greenhouse. Use them for jam, dry or open-freeze them on trays.

Pick mulberries when they are dark in colour and have a slight bloom. They make good jam and can be bottled or frozen.

The sharp-tasting yellow fruits of quince are too hard to eat raw, but they make good jelly and are delicious halved and baked like apples.

Harvesting VEGETABLES

Harvest pumpkins, such as the orange-skinned 'Mammoth', by cutting the stem with shears; leave a 5cm (2in) stub to prevent rot.

through the summer, as soon as they become large enough, but maincrop varieties mature in autumn.

Brassicas Summer cabbages should normally be harvested by early autumn. Many winter cabbages should also be cut before the heaviest frosts arrive, but other winter brassica crops are hardy enough to be left in the ground. Brussels sprouts may start cropping in early autumn, depending on variety. Cauliflowers must be harvested as soon as they are ready.

A well-planned vegetable garden should have some crops available for harvesting nearly all year round, but early autumn is the time when there is likely to be the maximum harvest.

SOME VEGETABLES can be left in the ground to be used through the autumn and winter; others need to be gathered and used (or stored) as soon as they reach maturity, or when frosts threaten.

Beans Both french and runner bean plants are sensitive to frost, and all beans remaining on the plants in early to mid-autumn should be picked before the first frost is likely.

Beetroot, carrots Young specimens of these root vegetables are harvested all

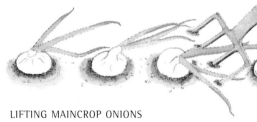

LIFTING MAINCROP ONIONS
When the first plants wilt, bend over the foliage of the whole row at the necks of the plants to help them ripen. A few days after this, prise up the roots with a fork and leave them to dry before storing.

Many maincrop varieties mature in autumn,

and leave them on the soil surface for a few hours to dry off before storing.

Squashes, marrows and courgettes Harvest all remaining fruits in early autumn, well before the first frost which will turn the plants to mush. Winter squashes and pumpkins are suitable for storage; others should be used up as soon as possible.

Sweet corn Most cobs are ready in early or mid-autumn, but pick sweet corn at the right stage for the best flavour. Harvest cobs before their liquid dries up and the kernels turn starchy.

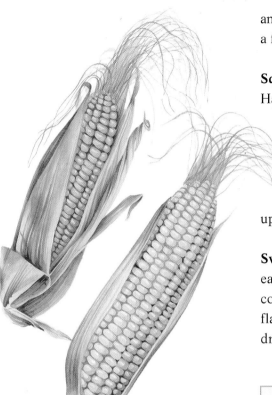

Twist off the ears of sweetcorn when the tassels are brown and withered and the seeds exude a milky juice.

Onions Prepare onions for harvest as soon as the foliage starts to turn yellow. Prise up the roots with a fork, leaving the onions lying on the surface of the soil to dry for a day or two, then lift and clean them for storing.

Potatoes Harvest maincrop potatoes in early to mid-autumn, during a dry, sunny spell. Lift the tubers with a garden fork but harvest them before frost arrives

Dig the soil deeply when harvesting potatoes, as it is surprising how many tubers may remain after the first forking up. Some potatoes are bound to be speared by the fork, and these should be used immediately.

Acorn squash is one of several winter squashes which store well if cut when mature. The skin is green or black and very hard and the orange flesh is solid in texture.

HARVESTING LEEKS

Leeks will keep on growing slowly during the winter, so lift only what you need, when the stems are about 2cm ($3/_4$in) thick. Ease plants out of the soil with a fork and cut off the roots, with the soil sticking to them, on the spot.

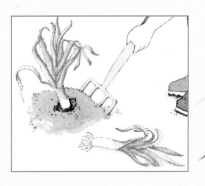

In light, sandy soils, carrots may be left in the ground through the winter, but in heavier soils they are prone to splitting and should be lifted and stored.

Storing VEGETABLES

Vegetables can be stored in a wide variety of ways during autumn to prolong their season of use.

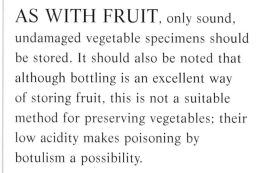

Autumn is a time of unrivalled abundance in the vegetable garden.

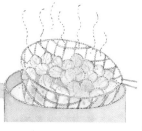

Blanching is the secret of freezing vegetables such as Brussels sprouts successfully. Plunge them into boiling water; keep the heat turned up so that the water returns to boiling rapidly and blanch for the correct time – 3–4 minutes in this case.

AS WITH FRUIT, only sound, undamaged vegetable specimens should be stored. It should also be noted that although bottling is an excellent way of storing fruit, this is not a suitable method for preserving vegetables; their low acidity makes poisoning by botulism a possibility.

Storing in the ground Many hardy vegetables can remain in the ground all winter, being harvested as required. Root vegetables are best in light, sandy soils; if there is very cold spell, it may be impossible to lift roots from the frozen soil, so it is a good idea to keep a small supply in a box. In heavy soils

there is a danger of roots splitting or rotting, in which case they are best lifted in late autumn for storing in a clamp or box, as below.

Storing in a clamp or box
A clamp is the traditional way to store root vegetables, but is not widely used these days. Place a thick layer of straw on some bare soil or paving in a sheltered part of the garden, or in a shed or cellar. Prepare root vegetables by twisting the foliage off where

necessary. Make a pyramid of roots on the straw and cover this with another layer of straw, then cover the whole with a layer of soil some 10–15cm (4–6in) deep, patting it down firmly with the back of a spade. Pull a twist of straw through the soil in a couple of places near the top of the heap for ventilation.

Storing vegetables in boxes of fine soil or sand in a cool area such as a garage or cellar is more convenient for most people. Prepare the roots as before and place them on a layer of sand or soil in a wooden or strong cardboard box, packing them in closely but not touching each other. Cover them completely with another layer of soil, and continue in layers until the box is full.

Lift beetroot in late autumn; twist or cut off the leaves 5cm (2in) above the bulbs and lay them in a box on sand or peat. Cover with another layer of sand or peat.

Freezing Many vegetables freeze well, especially runner, french and broad beans, sprouts, calabrese, cauliflower, peas and spinach.

Pickles and chutney Pickles use vinegar to prevent produce deteriorating; in the case of chutneys, sugar and vinegar are used, and the vegetables are mixed with fruit. Beetroot, cauliflower, courgette, cucumber, onion and red cabbage are commonly used in pickles, while recipes for chutney include those made from aubergine, marrow, onion, pepper, sweet corn and tomato.

Salting This method is sometimes used with good results for runner beans; it is especially useful if the freezer is full. Use a large stone or glass jar and place a layer of kitchen salt in the base. Prepare and slice the beans as if for cooking and place equal layers of beans and salt in the jar until full, topping with a layer of salt. Cover with a moisture-proof lid and store in a cool, dark place. Soak the beans in fresh water for two hours immediately before cooking.

Vegetables to sow now

The sowing season isn't over yet – suitable varieties of all these vegetables can be sown in autumn.

Broad bean
Calabrese
Carrot*
Cauliflower*
Chinese cabbage
Garlic (bulbs for planting)
Lettuce
Onion (sets for planting)
Pea
Radish
Rocket
Spinach
Overwinter in a cold frame

Onions keep well as long as they are completely ripe and dry before storage. The dead leaves can be plaited into ropes, or the onions can be placed in wooden, slatted boxes.

Kohl-rabi resembles a turnip in both appearance and flavour. Cook the leafy tops as cabbage; the fleshy stem, or bulb, is good in soups and stews.

Small bulbs with pale brown or silvery skins, pickling onions store well, or can be used as cocktail onions or preserved.

Plants for AUTUMN (1)

Autumn is a time of decline and decay in the garden, but it is also a season of exquisite beauty.

AT THE BEGINNING of autumn there are still many summer-flowering plants to be enjoyed, but as the season progresses, these are eclipsed by the brilliant foliage colours of deciduous trees and shrubs. Maples are among the best for autumn colour, but *Hamamelis* (witch hazel), *Malus* (crab apple), poplars, *Prunus* and *Sorbus* (mountain ash, rowan) all put on an excellent display. Some more unusual plants have their moment of glory in autumn, too: the leaves of *Liriodendron tulipifera* (tulip tree) turn glowing gold, *Liquidambar styraciflua* (sweet gum) has beautiful gold and crimson tints, and *Parrotia persica* takes on shades of yellow, crimson and orange.

The arresting colours of *Acer palmatum* are quintessentially autumnal and provide a ubiquitous highlight in gardens at this time of year.

Autumn

Malus 'John Downie' (crab apple). The early summer white flowers are followed in autumn by conical golden yellow fruits that cling to the branches well into winter.

Colourful autumn foliage has a spectacular but brief season before autumn gales bring the leaves down. Slightly longer lasting are the fruits and berries, including holly, *Pyracantha, Cotoneaster, Euonymous, Berberis, Skimmia...* there are all sizes, shapes and shades to enjoy.

The first sharp frost will put paid to the non-hardy bedding plants and perennials, but there are some plants that only begin to flower as the days get shorter and colder. *Schizostylis coccinea,* the kaffir lily, produces delicate-looking, cup-shaped flowers with a lovely satin texture to the petals, and among the bulbs, crinum, nerine and amaryllis put on a bold show of trumpet-shaped blooms in shades of pink and white. Other bulbs are in bloom now, too – autumn-flowering crocus, cyclamen and snowdrops among them.

Don't forget that many plants have attractive dead flowerheads or decorative seedheads for the autumn days. *Lunaria* (honesty) produces spikes of dull-looking, pale brown, flat pods, but when the papery covers are rubbed off, bright silver, translucent discs emerge. Poppies hold little, ribbed-top pepperpots on stiff stems, nigella has whiskery, inflated pods, and the papery, beige, faded flowers of hydrangeas have a pleasing shape and form. Take care not to spoil some of autumn's attractions by over-zealous deadheading in the border during the balmy days of late summer.

The highlight of autumn is the brilliant foliage colours of deciduous trees and shrubs

Many roses continue flowering throughout the autumn, and even on into winter in milder areas. These are three of the best to bring flower colour, fragrance and pleasing form at this time of the year.

Rosa 'Madame Alfred Carrière' is a quick grower in a shady site. Its large, fragrant blooms flourish well into the autumn.

Rosa 'Orange Sensation' is a small, cluster-flowered rose with a spreading habit. It has dark green glossy foliage and fragrant double blooms in early autumn.

Rosa 'Easter Morning' is a miniature rose with an upright habit. Its slightly fragrant, cup-shaped flowers are borne throughout the autumn.

Plants for AUTUMN (2)

After the glorious plant displays of spring and summer, expectations of autumn colour and interest may be low. Nothing could be further from the truth...

THERE ARE a surprising number of plants from nearly all categories which thrive during the autumn season, providing exceptional colour, form and fragrance as the year draws to a close. These are some of the best and most widely available.

Early autumn

Trees and shrubs

Abelia floribunda,
  A. x grandiflora
Buddleja davidii
Campsis radicans
Caryopteris x
  clandonensis
Ceanothus

Pyramid-shaped *Nyssa sylvatica* is a stunning sight in autumn, when its glossy, pointed leaves turn brilliant scarlet, red or orange.

Ceratostigma
Clematis species
  and hybrids
Clerodendrum
  bungei,
  C. trichotomum
Erica
Fuchsia
Hebe
Hibiscus syriacus
Hydrangea
  macrophylla
Hypericum
Indigofera
  heterantha
Leycesteria
  formosa
Perovskia
  atriplicifolia
Phygelius
Potentilla
Romneya coulteri
Rosa
Spartium junceum
Vinca major,
  V. minor
Yucca

Perennials and bedding plants

Achillea
Aconitum
  napellus
Anemone hybrida
Aster
Coreopsis
  verticillata
Eryngium
Helenium
Hemerocallis
Kniphofia
Nepeta faassenii
Rudbeckia
Schizostylis
  coccinea
Sedum spectabile
Solidago
Zauschneria
  californica

Bulbs

Amaryllis
  belladonna
Colchicum
Crinum powellii
Crocosmia
  crocosmiiflora
Crocus (autumn-
  flowering
  species)
Cyclamen
Lilium auratum,
  L. speciosum
Nerine bowdenii

Mid autumn

Trees and shrubs

Acer
Berberis
  (deciduous)
Callicarpa
  bodinieri
Calluna
Ceratostigma

The feathery flowerheads of *Solidago* 'Golden Wings' add colour to the border in early autumn, often crowding out other plants.

Cercidiphyllum
  japonicum
Clerodendrum
Cotinus coggygria
Cotoneaster
Erica
Euonymus alatus,
  E. europaeus
  and others
Fothergilla major

Pyracantha angustifolia's mass of berries.

Hamamelis
Hebe
Hippophae
  rhamnoides
Hydrangea
  quercifolia
Leycesteria
  formosa
Malus
Nyssa sylvatica
Parthenocissus
Pernettya
  mucronata
Pyracantha
Rosa moyesii,
  R. rubrifolia,
  R. rugosa
Skimmia

Sorbus
Symphoricarpos
Vaccinium
Viburnum
Vitis coignetiae,
   V. vinifera

Perennials
Aconitum
   napellus
Anemone hybrida
Aster
Gentiana sino-
   ornata
Kniphofia
Liriope muscari
Physalis
   franchettii
Sedum spectabile
Solidago

Bulbs
Amaryllis
   belladonna
Colchicum
Crinum powellii
Crocus (autumn-
   flowering
   species)
Cyclamen
Galanthus
   reginae-olgae

Rich autumn colours are the outstanding feature of *Parottia persica* (Persian ironwood).

Cyclamen hederifolium is a hardy, late-flowering bulbous plant that brightens the garden from late summer through to early winter.

Nerine bowdenii
Schizostylis
   coccinea

Late autumn

Trees and shrubs
Aucuba japonica
Berberis
Callicarpa
   bodinieri

Clematis
   orientale,
   C. tangutica
Cornus alba
Cotoneaster
Fatsia japonica
Gentiana sino-
   ornata
Jasminum
   nudiflorum
Leycesteria
   formosa
Malus
Pernettya
   mucronata
Prunus x
   subhirtella
   'Autumnalis'
Pyracantha
Rosa moyesii,
   R. rubrifolia,
   R. rugosa
Salix alba
   'Britzensis'
Skimmia

Sorbus
Symphoricarpos
Vaccinium
Viburnum

Perennials
Aster
Helianthus
Iris unguicularis
Liriope muscari

Bulbs
Colchicum
Crocus (autumn-
   flowering
   species)
Cyclamen
Galanthus
   reginae-olgae
Nerine bowdenii
Schizostylis
   coccinea
Sternbergia lutea

Iris unguicularis (Algerian iris) is a beardless iris which forms a large clump of grass-like evergreen foliage. It flowers throughout the autumn and winter, to early spring.

Lavatera trimestris 'Silver Cup' is a hardy, fast-growing annual with a bushy habit which flowers in summer and early autumn.

Nerine bowdenii flowers before the leaves appear.

Clockwise from top left:
Hamamelis mollis;
dogwood and winter
bulbs; frosty lawn;
poinsettia; *Physalis*;
winter grasses.

Winter

RENOVATION

Winter is the time to prepare for the new growing season that lies only just ahead, for each day there are reminders that spring is really not very far away. The fresh foliage of spring bulbs, such as grape hyacinths, can be seen spearing its way through the soil right from the earliest winter days, and the flowers of snowdrops and the first crocuses soon give a cheering foretaste of what is to come.

Take advantage of the quiet days of winter, when the garden is not overflowing with flowers and foliage, to reassess and replan the layout. It is generally easier to see where improvements could be made – and how to make them – at this time of year. The long, dark, cold evenings have their compensations, too, for one of the pleasantest occupations is to sit indoors in the warmth, dreaming and planning for the gardening year ahead.

Winter WINTER CHECKLIST

☑ In early winter begin digging over the vegetable garden and any bare patches of soil. Obtain a soil test kit to check acidity or alkalinity of the soil.

☑ Spread rotted compost or manure on vacant ground. Dig it into the soil or use as a mulch around established plants.

☑ Order bare-root trees and shrubs for delivery.

☑ Begin pruning fruit trees; this can continue throughout the winter.

☑ Bring forced bulbs into the home when the buds start to show colour.

☑ In midwinter order seeds and plan vegetable garden crops for next year.

☑ Knock snow off the branches of evergreens so that they do not break under its weight.

☑ Thaw ice on garden ponds to prevent toxic gases building up and harming fish.

☑ In late winter begin sowing seeds under cover.

☑ Send lawn mowers and other garden machinery away for servicing and blade sharpening before the spring rush.

☑ Remove weeds from flower borders and around shrubs and trees. Mulch the soil with chipped bark or similar.

☑ In the greenhouse start overwintering plants – such as fuchsias, and chrysanthemums – into growth by watering them and increasing the heat.

☑ Complete the planting of bare-root trees and shrubs before the new growing season starts.

Winter DIGGING

One of the most basic tasks in the garden – digging the soil over – is also one of the most beneficial, helping to rejuvenate the ground and to allow nourishment from the upper soil to penetrate down to where it will benefit the roots of your plants.

WHEREVER THERE IS bare soil over the winter – in the vegetable garden where crops have been cleared, or in the ornamental garden when annuals or bedding plants have been removed, for example – it is common practice to dig the ground over. There are several reasons for doing this.

• It enables all the debris from the crops to be cleared away.
• It allows the topgrowth and roots of weeds to be removed.
• It helps to break down the soil to fine crumbs, encouraging good root growth for subsequent plantings.
• It destroys any hard 'cap' that may have formed on the soil surface, or a 'pan' that may have formed lower down, and can improve both soil aeration and drainage.
• It allows organic matter and fertilizers to mix in thoroughly.

Soil types Soils which have a high clay content are more difficult to dig than light, sandy soils. The weather conditions must be just right for digging to take place; if it is too wet, the soil clings irritatingly to the blade of the spade, and each spadeful is heavy and awkward to handle. However, clay soils benefit even more from deep digging than light soils do, so it is worth persevering.

Winter digging is good for the garden and will pay dividends all the rest of the year. Soil needs renovating and recycling on a regular basis to give plants the nutrients they require in order to thrive.

When to dig Digging should take place as early in the winter as possible. There is no need to break up the clods of soil at this stage; as the winter progresses and frosts arrive in earnest, the action of the expanding ice shatters the clods naturally, and they will crumble away easily in spring. The earlier digging is done, the more chance the cold weather will have to work on the soil.

Large borders and vegetable plots may be too big to dig all at once, as digging is hard physical work. Do a bit at a time, whenever the soil is not actually frozen or very wet. Walking and working on wet soil compacts it, compressing the soil particles and squeezing out the air surrounding them. On free-draining soils it may be possible to dig at almost any stage of the winter, but on clay soils opportunities for cultivation are more restricted. If the soil clings to your boots in lumps when you walk across it – leave digging to another day. Apart from the structural damage caused to the soil, digging wet ground is too much like hard work, anyway.

The right tools The basic tool for digging is a spade. Choose one with a comfortable handle, that feels well balanced in your hands. A stainless steel blade sheds soil well, is easy to clean and lasts many years. The top of the blade should have a wide tread on which to place your foot to push the spade into the ground. In theory, the larger the spade, the more quickly the job should get done – but remember that each spadeful of soil will be heavier and more tiring, probably slowing down the work in the long run. For the less physically able, however, there are various brands of spade and adaptor handles you can buy which

> Wherever soil is bare during the winter, it is usual to dig the ground over thoroughly

make digging easier (see 'Digging without strain', page 152).

A mechanical cultivator is an excellent time- and labour-saving tool for turning over the top layer of soil, but it has its drawbacks. The depth reached by the tines is fairly shallow, and after several years of use a hard, impervious 'cultivation pan' can develop immediately below that. To prevent this happening, aim to deep dig the soil with a spade one year in three instead of using a mechanical cultivator. Cultivators are also difficult to handle on clay soils, tending to bounce off the hard surfaces, and sometimes require a lot of physical strength to control.

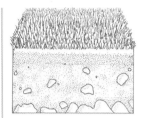

Ideal garden soil, or loam, is a mixture of sand, clay and humus. The darker its colour the more humus and nutrients it contains. Loam is even textured and crumbly when you rub it between your hands, and is ideal for most plants.

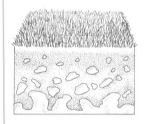

Chalky soil can be difficult to cultivate. It drains rather too well and the top-soil is shallow and low in nutrients, The addition of peat or humus improves the texture, helps retain moisture and reduces alkalinity.

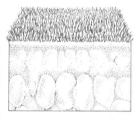

Clay is sticky and easily becomes waterlogged. It is rich, but must be drained and lightened by thorough digging and the addition of compost.

How to DIG

The digging regime you adopt is influenced by the type of soil you have, what you are trying to achieve – and your own physical capabilities.

You need to be reasonably fit to dig effectively. Do not overdo things when you first begin turning the soil.

WINTER DIGGING can be backbreaking physical labour. Using the correct techniques will ensure that you don't damage either the soil structure or your own health.

Avoiding back trouble Unless you are particularly fit, tackle digging a little at a time; do a few minutes a day, and take small spadefuls of soil. Lever the soil out of the trench rather than lifting it, and allow the spadeful of soil to slide off the blade. Keep your spine as straight as possible and try to use your knees for bending.

If you find digging difficult for any reason, try using a fork instead. You can also buy an auxiliary handle to fit on the shaft of the spade to help with lifting it, or a special spring-loaded spade that throws the soil off the blade automatically.

Digging methods There are three main methods of digging.

Turning or forking: this can be done with either a spade or a fork, which is driven in to the full depth of the blade (a spit). The soil is then turned over and dropped back into the same position. This is a quick method, useful on light, well-drained soils, or where only small or restricted areas require digging over.

Single digging: this is suitable for a fairly large expanse of vacant soil, such as a vegetable plot. Dig out a straight-sided trench one spit deep and about 30cm (12in) wide, and put the soil in a wheelbarrow. Moving backwards, dig out a similar trench immediately behind it, throwing the soil from this forwards into the first trench. (Any organic matter that is being incorporated should be mixed with the soil as it goes back.) Use the barrowful of soil from the first trench to fill in the last one.

Double digging: this is carried out in the same way as single digging, but fork over the soil at the base of the trench to the depth of one spit before refilling it as before. This means the soil is cultivated to two spits depth instead of one, as with single digging.

Winter

Digging without strain
Take it slowly if you are not used to digging or have not done any for some time – start with about half an hour a day. Drive in the blade of the spade at right angles to the trench; lift the soil just clear of the ground, tilting the blade. Work rhythmically, letting the weight and momentum of the spade and your own weight pressing on it do most of the work.

SINGLE DIGGING

Press down on top of the blade with your foot, using the edge of the trench as a fulcrum. The soil from the first trench goes into a barrow to fill the final trench. Step back, and fill the first trench with the soil from the second, and so on. Twist the spade as you throw the soil forward to invert it and bury annual weeds; remove perennial weeds. Mix in compost or manure as you work.

An alternative to digging Soil compaction, and bringing a new crop of weed seeds to the surface, are detrimental side effects of digging. Some gardeners prefer to establish a no-dig or deep-bed system, especially for vegetable growing, and it is favoured by organic gardeners.

After an initial double digging, and adding large amounts of organic matter, small beds surrounded by pathways are formed, so that the beds can be reached from all sides without being walked over. Organic matter is added annually to the beds in the form of a deep mulch, which is incorporated naturally.

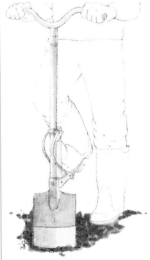

If you find digging too difficult, you could try using an automatic, spring-loaded spade (see above). This works with a lever action, almost eliminating lifting and bending. The blade is hinged to a footplate, so a pull on the handlebars throws the soil forward into the trench, turning it over at the same time.

DOUBLE DIGGING

Double digging is useful on heavy, badly drained soils, or where a hard cultivation pan has formed below the first spit. Because it is hard work, it is usually carried out only when cultivating a piece of land for the first time, or if necessary after a number of years of continued cultivation. Only the fit and vigorous should consider undertaking double digging.

 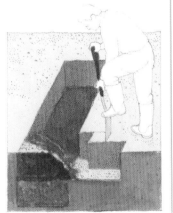

Testing THE SOIL

Getting to know your soil is one of the most important things you should do before rushing out and spending money on plants that don't have a hope of thriving in the conditions you have in your garden.

Different plants prefer – or need – different types of soil. Wildflower meadows such as the one pictured here are generally a feature of chalky soil, in which poppies, daisies, speedwell and the like will flourish.

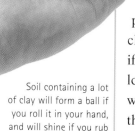

Soil containing a lot of clay will form a ball if you roll it in your hand, and will shine if you rub it with your thumb.

SOIL PLAYS a very important part in the growth of plants, and it is worth taking the trouble to find out as much as you can about the soil in your garden.

Dig out a trowelful of moist soil and squeeze it in the palm of your hand. Soil that crumbles and will not form a cohesive ball has a high proportion of sand, while soil that clings together contains more clay. See if you can roll it into a ball, then into a long snake; try to join the ends together without the ring breaking. The more of these things the soil will do, the higher the percentage of clay it contains.

Another useful test is to add some soil to a screw-top glass jar and half-fill it with plain water. Put on the lid and shake the jar vigorously for a few minutes, then leave it overnight to settle. It will separate out into distinct layers. The heaviest constituents – the small stones and grit – will be on the bottom, with a layer of coarse sand on top of that, continuing up the glass to the finest particles, the clays and silts, as the top layer, with organic matter floating on the surface of the water. A quick glance will show you the varying proportions of the different constituents that make up the soil in your garden, or part of your garden.

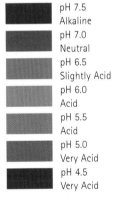

2

4

	pH 7.5 Alkaline
	pH 7.0 Neutral
	pH 6.5 Slightly Acid
	pH 6.0 Acid
	pH 5.5 Acid
	pH 5.0 Very Acid
	pH 4.5 Very Acid

5

CHECKING THE pH CONTENT OF SOIL

1 Most kits consist of a container for the soil sample, a dropper, capsules of chemicals and a chart. 2 Take a soil sample 5–7.5cm (2–3in) below the surface. Put one chemical capsule into the tester; add two capsules of dried soil and distilled water. 3 Make sure it comes up to the dotted line, then fit the cap and shake the tester well. 4 Let it stand for a few minutes to allow the colour to develop fully. 5 Against a white background, in natural daylight, but not sunlight, compare the coloured solution with the colours on the chart. This will tell you whether your soil is alkaline or acid.

Light, sandy soils are free-draining and are unlikely to become waterlogged; they warm up quickly in the spring and are easy to work. They may suffer from water shortage in dry weather, and also nutrient shortages, as soluble nutrients are easily washed away. Clay soils become compacted easily; they are slow to warm up, difficult to work and prone to waterlogging. On the other hand, they do not dry out as quickly as sandy soils, and contain more plant nutrients. The structure of both light and heavy soils is greatly improved by the addition of well-rotted organic matter such as manure or garden compost.

Chemical testing kits Soil-testing kits are available from most garden centres. Some kits include tests for nitrogen, potassium and phosphorous as well as the pH test, which is the most accurate and will tell you the acidity or alkalinity of your soil. Take samples from different areas of the garden and test them separately for the most accurate results. For a more detailed assessment of the soil's pH and nutrient status, you will need to send a sample to a commercial laboratory for testing.

The acidity level of the soil is important for some plants, which will not grow in alkaline conditions. These are known as calcifuges, or lime-haters, and include members of the Ericaceae family, such as heathers, as well as such popular plants as rhododendrons.

Acid-loving plants are among the most decorative in the garden. They all need acid, moisture-retentive but well-drained soil.

Kalmia latifolia (calico bush, mountain laurel) is a charming evergreen shrub with clusters of unusually shaped clear pink flowers.

Pieris 'Forest Flame' is a highly ornamental, dense evergreen shrub with foliage that changes from bright pink in spring to cream and finally green.

Meconopsis grandis (blue poppy) with its striking flowers, prefers some acidity in the soil. It is short-lived, and often only biennial.

Making GARDEN COMPOST

Grass cuttings are the mainstay of most gardener's compost heaps, but more open-textured material is needed as well in order to prevent the compost heap becoming too dense and airless.

ALL GARDEN SOILS benefit from the addition of rotted organic matter, and as much as possible should be incorporated during winter digging. This type of soil improver is often referred to as 'bulky organic matter' – and bulky it certainly is. Unlike concentrated fertilizers, which are sprinkled by the handful, organic matter should be applied in barrowloads. This means that suitable substances are awkward to buy, store and transport. Depending on the area in which you live, you may be able to obtain spent mushroom compost, spent hops, treated sewage waste and farmyard or stable manure; these are excellent but by no means readily available to all gardeners. There is one easy answer, and that is to make garden compost. It is a very valuable organic soil improver which costs nothing to make, and it disposes of garden waste that can otherwise be difficult to get rid of.

Compost bins Plant material will rot down in almost any sort of heap, but containing it makes it look tidier and speeds up the process. Air, moisture and warmth are the three essentials. An ideal compost bin has enough ventilation to supply sufficient air, but not so much that all the heat escapes. Slatted wood bins are

excellent: chicken wire stretched around four sturdy posts will work well, but rotting will be quicker if three sides are lined with cardboard from flattened cartons or similar. There are also plenty of proprietary bins of various styles. Large bins are much more efficient than small ones: make the base at least 1m (3ft) square. Ideally, make two bins side by side, so that one can be rotting down while the other is being filled.

Garden waste Almost any plant material can be put on a compost heap, but it should be well mixed for best results. Dense materials, such as grass clipppings, must be mixed with more open material to prevent it forming a compacted airless mass, while woody waste, such as prunings, should be shredded to reduce its bulk before being composted.

Avoid adding weeds which have spreading roots, such as couch grass, or which are seeding. In a perfectly made compost heap, the high temperature will kill them off, but few heaps are perfect. It is also best to avoid adding plant material that is infected with diseases, particularly virus diseases, to prevent the infection being spread around the garden. Diseased material needs to be got rid of permanently and, ideally, should be burned.

Garden compost is a very valuable organic soil

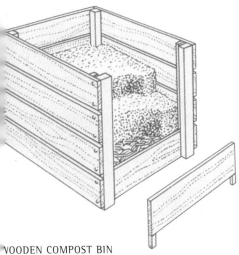

WOODEN COMPOST BIN
This type of wooden bin is easy to make. The slatted sides allow air to circulate freely, an important factor in helping the compost to rot down properly.

Kitchen waste Most vegetable trimmings and peelings will compost satisfactorily, although tough material such as grapefruit skins will take a long time to break down. Chopping them into

small pieces before adding them to the compost will help to speed up the process. Eggshells also take a long time to disappear, so crush them first. Do not add cooked food, plate scrapings or meat products, since these will attract vermin and also smell unpleasant while they are decomposing. Keep a lidded plastic bin by the kitchen door for compostable waste, to cut down the number of trips you have to make to the compost heap.

It is useful to add an occasional layer of garden soil to the waste matter as it builds up in the heap – this encourages the bacteria that are responsible for decomposition. Turning the heap from time to time is also an excellent idea, though often rather difficult to manage. When the bin is full, it should be left to rot down until it has formed a dark, crumbly, odourless material – this usually takes between three and six months.

Garden compost is especially beneficial in the vegetable garden and, in turn, some vegetables add nutrients to the soil.

When broad beans have been harvested, cut off the main stems of the plants at ground level and put them on the compost heap. Leave the roots in the ground to help add to the soil's fertility.

ALTERNATIVE COMPOSTERS
In the container on the left new composting material goes in on the top, and slats at the front can be raised to allow the mature compost to be taken out from the base. The one on the right has the advantage that it can be spun, allowing the compost to be circulated.

In winter, dig plenty of compost into the soil where beans are to grow. They are greedy feeders, but, like other legumes, add nitrogen to the soil.

improver which costs nothing to make

Making GARDEN COMPOST **157**

Clearing FLOWER BORDERS

When many plants in the garden are dead or dying, there is a great temptation to have a big clear-out. However, be careful what you remove in winter.

Winter is the time to make decisions about your flower borders – what needs to go and what can stay.

APART FROM ONE or two very late-flowering plants, the display from most perennial flower borders is well and truly over by early winter. The dead growth often makes a rather depressing sight, and tidying the borders in early winter improves the appearance of the garden. It also cuts down overwintering sites for slugs and snails, and a range of other pests and diseases.

Dead and dying stems and flower-heads should be cut down to the base of the plant with shears or secateurs, and taken to the compost heap; any weed growth around the plants should also be removed. Stakes and other plant supports can be taken up, cleaned and stored away for the following year.

Not all perennials should be cut back, however. For example, some plants, such as *Nigella*, poppies,

The deep purple leaves of *Heuchera* 'Palace Purple' remain throughout the winter, and in summer the plant bears tall sprays of tiny white flowers.

Chinese lanterns, *acanthus* and hydrangea, have dead flowers or seedheads that remain attractive through the winter. Their russet-brown colours and contrasting outlines add interest to the winter garden scene, especially when they are rimed with frost on cold mornings.

Then there are the plants which, unlike most perennials, are evergreen – or at least, partially evergreen in the right situation. The large foliage of bergenias, tinged with magenta, and heuchera, with its purple or white-marbled, crinkle-edged leaves, are excellent examples of plants that should persist well into the winter, though they may start to look a little the worse for wear as the season wears on.

Finally, there are the plants that actually produce their flowers in winter. Hellebores, already valuable for their foliage, also bear striking winter blooms in shades of green, white or purple. The lilac-coloured flowers of *Liriope muscari* (lilyturf) will persist into winter and, at the other end of the season, there is the little *Adonis*, whose golden flowers, backed by a distinctive green ruff, liven up the later days of winter.

These plants should have any damaged or yellowed leaves removed during the winter season, and be staked if necessary to display them attractively. Clearing away dead and dying foliage and flowers from the other border plants around them will ensure that they take centre stage.

Sometimes dead plant stems can be visually appealing and should be left. There is a forlorn beauty to these rusty, bare allium seedheads.

Many alpines are perennials and can withstand winter cold and rain, provided that they are planted in well-drained soil.

The Universal Series of pansies is fully hardy and produces flowers ranging from bright jewel colours to pastels right through winter into spring.

Gentiana septemfida (gentian) is a hardy perennial evergreen that blooms in late summer and autumn.

Dianthus deltoides (maiden pink) flowers during the summer, but the mound of grey-green leaves remains attractive in winter.

Tool MAINTENANCE

Take time over the winter months to give all your garden tools a careful inspection, and clean, sharpen and replace them as necessary.

A well-maintained collection of tools makes a gardener's life much easier, and you should store them carefully in the dry and lay them out in a way that makes them readily accessible.

WINTER, WHEN there is not so much to do in the garden, is an ideal time for carrying out maintenance work on tools and equipment, particularly those items which are likely to be stored away until the spring.

Maintenance of hand tools Tools should be cleaned each time they are used, but early winter is a good time to give them a really thorough cleaning, using emery paper or wire wool to

A versatile weed and hoe tool. This one is on a detachable head that clips on to a full-length shaft.

These days you can buy weeding tools with interchangeable heads for different purposes.

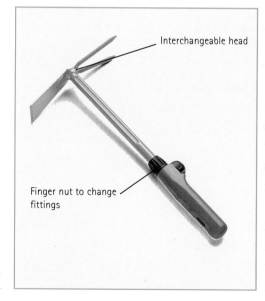

Interchangeable head

Finger nut to change fittings

Wooden shafts of rakes, hoes, spades and forks may need fine sandpaper to smooth them and remove splinters; if necessary the shafts can be renewed completely. Cut off the old shaft close to the tool head, then place the tool head in the centre of a bonfire for several hours to help remove all

Tools should be correctly stored to ensure they have a long life

traces of the shaft from within the socket. Take care to let it cool completely before handling it.

Tools should be correctly stored to ensure they have a long life. A clean, dry shed is ideal, with tools preferably hung up on racks on the shed walls. This makes them easier to find when they are required, and ensures they are not damaged or stored in damp conditions.

When carrying out winter maintenance of hand tools, make a note of those that need replacing now or in the near future. Working with worn-out or badly designed tools makes any job twice as difficult, and buying new, well-made, comfortable replacements is always a worthwhile investment.

remove stubborn deposits or areas of rust. The blades of tools such as pruning knives, Dutch hoes and spades should be sharpened to keep them working efficiently, and you can usually do this yourself, using a file or a carborundum stone. Cutting tools such as shears or secateurs, however, are best sent away for professional sharpening. Stainless steel tools cannot be sharpened.

After cleaning, the metal parts of tools should be given a light coating of oil to protect them from damp, and moving parts of all tools should also be oiled to keep them working freely.

Tool handles need to be comfortable to use and the right ones for the job.

The traditional D-shape used to be a popular shape for wooden hilts.

T-shaped handles were generally used with wooden shafts, but are now considered old-fashioned.

The YD shape – either in plastic or in wood – is now considered the strongest for modern tools.

Machinery MAINTENANCE

If you've paid out for garden machinery – and some of it can cost quite considerable sums of money – then it's particularly important to maintain it, and to store it securely.

Lawnmowers and other garden machinery require regular maintenance, which might include stripping down.

MOST GARDENERS use at least some items of powered machinery – lawn mowers, hedge trimmers, cultivators, shredders, nylon line trimmers and chainsaws are the most popular pieces of equipment. Regular maintenance is essential to keep these in good, safe running order.

Machinery may be powered by electricity or a petrol engine.

Electric tools Most electrical equipment needs little maintenance, but some safety checks are essential. During an annual winter check, make sure that the plug is not cracked or damaged and is correctly wired and fitted with the right fuse. The flex should be checked for splits or frayed areas, and replaced where necessary. Make sure that the residual current device is operating.

Petrol engines Types of engine vary from one machine to another, so always read the manual for detailed maintenance instructions. For most petrol engines, the following tasks should be carried out before storing equipment away for the winter.

Drain the petrol tank and run the engine until it stops, to ensure that

Winter

here is no petrol in the carburettor. Clean the machine thoroughly and give metal parts a coating of oil; apply grease to grease nipples and lubricate cables. Leave the engine on compression by slowly pulling the starter cord (if fitted) until you feel resistance; this closes the valves to prevent rusting in the cylinder and the valves sticking open when you first try to start the engine the following spring.

In late winter, service the engine. Clean spark plugs and reset the gap using feeler gauges, or replace plugs if necessary. If contact breakers are fitted, these can also be cleaned and the gap reset, though contact breakers are less accessible than spark plugs. Run the engine until hot and change the oil. Adjust the tension of drive chains or belt if present; lubricate chains and check the belt for wear. It may also be necessary to adjust the fuel mixture and tickover speed after winter storage.

If you do not feel inclined to carry out the service yourself, book the machine in to a reliable dealer – but make sure you

Keep garden tools and machinery well oiled and greased, particularly if they are stored in a garden shed or outhouse. Rust and mechanical seizure are common problems with many tools and machines.

do this at the beginning of the winter, rather than at the end.

Other maintenance Clean all machinery thoroughly, removing soil, grass and rust. Check that the blades of a cylinder mower are correctly adjusted – see how cleanly they cut a piece of paper. If the mower has not been cutting well, send the cylinder away for sharpening or regrinding. Otherwise adjust the cylinder so the blades just 'kiss' the fixed blade and coat each blade with grease. Rotary mower blades may also need to be resharpened.

Nylon line trimmers should have dead grass and debris removed from around the reel; the nylon line is replaced as soon as it has run out. Lubricate the blades and reciprocating mechanism of a hedge trimmer with oil, and send it to a specialist if sharpening is required. Chain saws should also be sent away for resharpening; it is vital to check that the chain is correctly tensioned, since a slack chain can be dangerous.

Lastly, store all garden machinery and equipment in a dry, secure place; electrical equipment, in particular, will not function properly if it becomes damp.

Always use outdoor cables, plugs and circuit breakers with electrical tools and machines in the garden. If in doubt, do not buy the tool.

Electric strimmers are now an everyday item of garden equipment. They require attentive care and maintenance, like all electrical machines.

Winter CARE OF LAWNS

Looking after your lawn during the winter will pay dividends once the grass starts growing again, so don't neglect it at this time of year.

IN MOST YEARS, grass stops growing during the winter, and the lawn mower can be serviced and stored away. On some occasions, though, winters are mild enough for the grass to need mowing once or twice in the course of the season. This should be done during a fine, dry spell, and the grass only needs to be lightly topped. Fallen leaves should not be allowed to lie on the grass, but should be raked or brushed away with a stiff broom or besom as they occur throughout the winter months. A leaf sweeper or blower will make the job quicker and easier on a large area of grass.

In wet or frosty weather, it is important to keep off the lawn as far as possible. Walking on wet turf compacts it, damaging the growth of the grass;

Wintry conditions can plague lawns and border plants even well outside the normal limits of the season. This frosty garden was actually photographed in mid-May – that is, in late spring/early summer!

In wet or frosty weather, it is important to

Where lawns fail to thrive, you can replace the grass with other forms of groundcover plant. Evergreen types effective in winter include:

Ajuga (bugle)
Bergenia
Calluna and *Erica* (heather, heath)
Hebe
Juniperus (juniper)
Pachysandra
Polygonum (knotweed)
Tiarella (foam flower)
Vinca (periwinkle)

walking on frozen grass will kill the leaves, creating a tell-tale trail of black footprints. If there is a frequently used route running across the lawn, it is a good idea to lay a firm path or stepping stones to avoid wear on the grass in cold and wet weather. In summer, the turf may be able to cope with the traffic, but in winter, a pathway soon becomes evident as grass dies out, leaving a muddy track. A temporary path of planks or netting can

The value of ornamental grasses in the winter garden is great. Many late-flowering varieties are stunning when their feathery tops are lit up by slanting winter sunshine.

be used to protect the turf in the short term – if manure or compost has to be barrowed over the lawn to the vegetable garden, for example.

Worn, obviously compacted areas of grass should be spiked as soon as they are noticed, driving a garden fork deeply into the lawn and moving it backwards and forwards before withdrawing it (see page 111). General repairs can continue in mild spells all through the winter, although the coldest midwinter days are best avoided.

Make use of the slack days of winter to service and maintain lawn-care tools and equipment (see pages 160–3). Sharpen half-moon edging irons and lawn shears; give the mower its annual overhaul and ensure the blades are sharpened and well adjusted before the new mowing season begins.

At a time when the grass on your lawn isn't actively growing, and not looking at its best either, ornamental grasses can liven up a winter garden. Many are fully hardy and resistant to frost.

Cortaderia selloana (pampas grass) is a striking, frost-hardy plant that stands out dramatically in a winter garden. It can grow to a height of 2.5m (8ft).

Pennisetum orientale is another plant which offers dramatic form in an otherwise barren winter garden. It has a round, bushy habit and, given some protection, will thrive in cold, unforgiving conditions.

keep off the lawn as far as possible

The VEGETABLE GARDEN

In midwinter there's still plenty to do, from harvesting winter vegetables to preparing new vegetable patches for the coming season, as well as sitting down with seed catalogues and deciding which new varieties you will try.

Frost may grip the vegetable garden, but there is still plenty to do to prepare for spring.

Some vegetables, such as Brussels sprouts, are thought to have a better flavour after frosting. Pick only those you need, and leave the rest to mature on the plant.

WINTER DIGGING of spare ground should continue in the vegetable garden, but there should also be crops to harvest right through until next season. Brassicas, such as cabbages and brussels sprouts, often need protection from pigeons during the winter; netting or fleece does a good job.

Winter is the time to plan vegetable growing for the following year. Take into account the performance of this year's crops, dropping those that did not do well or were not popular with the family, instead try out something new. Start browsing through the seed catalogues as soon as they arrive (see page 178).

For the best yields, practise a yearly rotation of crops in the vegetable plot; this avoids the build-up of specific pests and diseases and helps prevent nutrient shortages in the soil. Vegetables are classified into three main groups – root crops, brassicas, and peas and beans. Root crops include vegetables such as parsnips, potatoes, carrots and beetroot. Brassicas means all types of cabbages, sprouts, calabrese, cauliflower and so on; swedes, radishes and turnips go here (even

ROOT CROPS	BRASSICAS	PEAS AND BEANS
• Parsnips • Potatoes • Carrots • Beetroot • Leeks • Salsify • Celery * Aubergines • Shallots • Florence fennel • Tomatoes	• Cabbages • Sprouts • Calabrese • Cauliflower • Swedes • Radish • Turnips • Spinach • Kale • Broccoli • Chinese cabbage	• French beans •Marrow • Lettuce • Swiss chard • Dwarf beans • Onions •Runner beans • Chicory • Globe artichokes • Peas

Winter produces its distinctive crop, particularly root vegetables, which have stored up goodness below the ground during the summer.

Carrots will be difficult to remove from frozen soil, so if frosts threaten dig them up and keep them in a box of sand or soil in a shed.

VEGETABLE CROP ROTATION

The vegetable plot is split into three beds, one for each group. In succeeding years, brassicas are grown in the plot that was previously occupied by peas and beans, root crops move into the brassica's old bed, leaving peas and beans to grow in the bed that held root crops. After three years, each group is back where it started.

though they are also root crops), and so does spinach (which is not a brassica but has similar nutritional requirements to them). Along with the peas and beans go the miscellaneous crops that do not fit into the other two groups, such as lettuces, marrows and onions.

A strict rotation is often difficult to put into practice because of the difficulty of growing equal amounts of vegetables in each group, the lack of space available and so on, but try to follow the guidelines as far as possible.

Late winter is a good time to plant shallots, and early peas and broad beans can be sown outdoors. 'Aquadulce Claudia' is the broad bean for winter sowing; among the peas, choose round-seeded varieties such as 'Feltham First' or 'Meteor'.

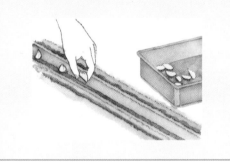

PLANTING GARLIC AND SHALLOTS

Plant garlic (above) by making a drill about 4cm (1½in) deep with a hoe, then set the cloves in it 10cm (4in) apart. Plant shallots (below) in a shallow hole with all but the tip of the bulb buried. Protect them from birds.

If turnips are left in the ground they will produce a crop of green leaves in early spring, which can be used like spring greens.

Parsnips will survive a frost, so can be left in the ground for the winter, and dug up for use as they are needed. Use in soups and stews, as well as roasting.

Pruning FRUIT TREES

Cutting fruit trees back correctly is the best way of ensuring that the tree puts its energy into producing fruit, rather than simply generating new wood.

Long-handled loppers are invaluable for cutting higher branches and those too thick for secateurs.

THE WINTER PRUNING of apples and pears often appears a skilled and mysterious art to novice fruit growers, but it need not be. The purpose of pruning is to keep the tree to a manageable size and shape, and to encourage the maximum crop of fruit.

Pruning of apples and pears can be carried out at any time in the dormant season except when it is very frosty, but it is best to get the job done as early in the winter as convenient. (Remember that plum trees should not be pruned in winter because of the risk of silver leaf disease.) Always use a sharp, clean pair of secateurs and make pruning cuts just above a bud, with the cut sloping away from the bud. Sealing compounds which were once used on large pruning cuts are no longer considered helpful and are unnecessary.

Most apple and pear trees in gardens are grown as open-centred bushes. The aim when pruning these should be to maintain a fruitful, well-balanced, goblet-shaped tree. Many older garden fruit trees are over-vigorous, producing excessive strong, leafy growth, and the temptation is to prune these back hard in winter. This must be avoided, however, since hard winter pruning only encourages even more vigorous growth next spring. Summer pruning will help to control their vigour, but where space for a fruit tree is limited,

Rows of pear trees in a commercial orchard, heavy with blossom, are evidence of the value of correct pruning.

it may be best to start again, replacing old trees with new, dwarf bush trees on a dwarfing rootstock.

Both apples and pears usually produce fruit in clusters on short,

Pruning can often appear to be a skilled and

TYPES OF GROWTH

To prune a fruit tree for the best results, identify the different types of growth. Prune bush trees in winter to stimulate growth, and trained trees in summer to retard their growth.

(1) Leader (2) Fruiting spur

(3) Smaller growth bud (4) Lateral shoot

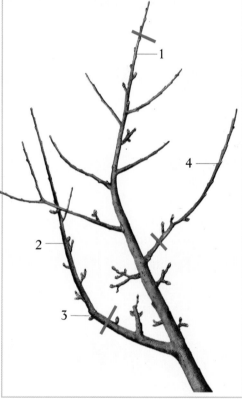

'Beauty of Bath' is a tip-bearing tree that produces fine, sweet dessert apples early in the season.

Late flowering and so avoiding frost, 'Lady Sudeley' is a soft, juicy dessert apple – yellow flushed with scarlet – which ripens in late summer.

'Laxton's Superb' bears a good crop of red-streaked yellow-green apples late in the autumn, but usually only in alternate years.

stumpy shoots called spurs, which are carried on wood that is at least two years old. However, a few varieties are tip bearers; here the fruit is borne at the ends of shoots which grew the previous summer. These need to be pruned in a different way to spur-bearing varieties to avoid removing all the fruit-bearing wood. Tip-bearing apples include 'Beauty of Bath', 'Lady Sudeley', 'Ellison's Orange', 'Worcester Pearmain', 'Bess Pool' and 'Laxton's Superb'; 'Josephine de Malines' and 'Jargonelle' are tip-bearing pears. Fruit tree catalogues should indicate which varieties are tip bearers.

mysterious art, but it need not be so

Pruning BUSH FRUIT TREES

Following the basic principles of spur and renewal pruning will ensure a healthy and successful tree.

THE FIRST STEP with all types of pruning is to remove all dead, diseased and dying wood, cutting it right back to healthy tissue. Next, remove crossing branches, which congest the growth and will rub against each other when they are weighed down with fruit.

Remove inward-facing sideshoots to leave the centre of the tree open. From this point, there are two main types of pruning method; spur pruning and renewal pruning, with a slightly different method for tip-bearing varieties. It is important to be able to distinguish between fruit buds and growth buds, particularly when pruning tip bearers. Growth buds are smooth, slender and pointed, while fruit buds are plump, squat and covered in a light, grey down.

For most bush trees, a mixture of spur and renewal pruning is used, with spur pruning taking place on the inside of the tree and renewal pruning on the outer branches.

Spur pruning The tips of branches and young sideshoots are cut back to stimulate the formation of fruiting spurs. Cut back branch leaders by up to one-third – less on vigorous varieties – in order to promote the formation of new sideshoots. Cut existing sideshoots (laterals) back to between three and six buds to encourage the formation of fruiting spurs.

On older trees, established spur systems will have formed and may become overcrowded. If so, thin these out, removing the weakest spurs and leaving younger, stronger ones.

Renewal pruning This encourages the production of a proportion of strong young wood each year to replace older, worn-out fruiting wood. Begin the procedure by leaving sideshoots unpruned in their first winter. By the following winter, fruit buds will have formed on the older wood, and the new growth that has been made during the

Early spring, when the flower buds are beginning to swell, is the best time to evaluate the success of your winter pruning. A well-pruned tree, such as this bush apple, will have an open, goblet shape so that light and air can reach the crown.

TOOLS FOR PRUNING

Useful tools (along with a pruning knife, secateurs and long-handled loppers) are a pruning saw and short loppers. Make sure they are kept sharp so that you cut cleanly; you don't want to damage the tree.

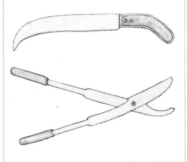

'St Edmund's Russet' is borne on both spurs and the tips of branches. It is a small, pale yellow dessert apple which, when ripe, turns gold.

RENOVATING AN APPLE TREE

A neglected apple tree before pruning (above left) will be tall and congested, with a great deal of twiggy growth. It can be rejuvenated by removing dead wood, any crossing branches, vertical branches and excessive thin growth. The end result of your labours (below left) should be a more open framework of branches and a good crop of fruit within a year or two.

A large, green cooking apple that turns yellow as it ripens, 'Grenadier' has fine-flavoured flesh and is crisp and acid.

summer is pruned off. By the third winter, the shoot will have carried a crop of fruit, and can be cut right back to within 2.5cm (1in) or so of its base. A new lateral will then be produced from this base, which will allow you to repeat the process.

Tip bearers These need only light pruning. Cut out a proportion of older wood which has already carried fruit and then tip back branch leaders. This will encourage the formation of sideshoots, which will carry fruit the following year.

'Worcester Pearmain' is a tip bearer, producing good, regular crops of bright red fruits that are crisp and juicy if ripened on the tree.

Coping with SNOW AND ICE

Don't leave your garden to the mercy of the cold and snows of winter – you can do a lot to protect it.

SNOW CAN GIVE useful protection to plants, acting as an insulating blanket to protect them from extreme cold. It can also, however, do a lot of damage. Because snow looks so light and fluffy it is easy to forget just how heavy wet snow really is, and it is

This lawn has been mowed in a attractive chequered pattern, enhanced by the heavy frost, but beware – walking on it in this state could kill the grass.

certainly enough to break branches on shrubs and trees.

Evergreen plants are most at risk, because the foliage presents a larger surface area for the snow to lie on, allowing it to build up to dangerous levels. Immediately after moderate snowfall, it is wise to go out and knock the snow from the branches of evergreens with a broom handle or something similar; the branches may

often be weighed down to the ground but will usually spring back up again if the snow is removed promptly. Leaving the snow where it is increases the risk of branches snapping, especially if there is a further snowfall.

In areas where snow can be expected in most winters, it is a sensible precaution to prepare a slender, upright conifer by tying strong twine around the tree in two or three places, or using a piece of netting to surround it. This will prevent branches being splayed out by the weight of snow, which can permanently ruin the tree's shape.

In freezing weather, fish in garden ponds can be at particular risk. This is not because of the

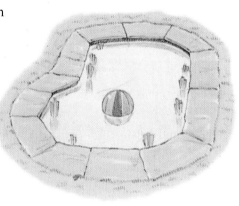

A ball can absorb the expansion of the ice, which might otherwise crack the pond walls.

cold temperatures, but because the layer of ice seals the pond and prevents any exchange of air at the water surface. Gases given off naturally by plant and fish waste products in the water cannot escape, and are likely to build up to toxic levels. If the water has been frozen for more than a day, a hole should be melted in the ice to allow gases to escape. Stand a metal saucepan or empty tin filled with boiling water on the ice, refilling it as necessary until a hole has been formed.

> Snow can give useful protection to plants... it can also, however, do a lot of damage.

Do not try to break the ice forcibly, since the shock waves are harmful to fish. An electric pond heater will keep an area clear of ice at all times and is cheap to buy and run.

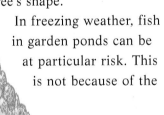

The weight of snow can easily snap branches on conifers, so if heavy snowfalls are likely to occur in your area, it is a good idea to tie in the branches with rope on any trees that are at risk.

Several common ferns, such as *Nephrolepis exaltata* (sword fern) and *Polypodium vulgare*, are evergreen, and can withstand all but the most severe weather.

Mahonia x 'Charity' is a winter delight. It bears racemes of deep yellow, sweet-scented flowers all through the coldest months.

Even under frost, the low mounds of grey foliage of hardy *Santolina* (cotton lavender) are attractive.

Wind Protection for PLANTS

Wind can cause physical damage to your garden, as well as drying out your trees and plants, so you need to take steps to protect the most vulnerable of them.

WIND CAN DAMAGE plants in two ways. First, there is the physical damage such as broken stems, torn leaves and root rock; secondly there is the desiccating effect of wind on the foliage. Evergreens are most vulnerable to damage. The presence of a full complement of leaves throughout the winter means intensifies the drying effects of wind; foliage also presents more resistance to wind, so that plants are more likely to be blown over or have their roots disturbed. Newly planted specimens which have not had time to become established are at particular risk.

Windbreaks are barriers designed to cut down the damaging effects of wind on plants. If a garden is in an exposed position where strong winds are a frequent occurrence, a permanent windbreak is useful; if protection is required for just a short time – while a new shrub gets established, for example – , temporary windbreaks such as a length of windbreak netting are all that is required.

When building a permanent windbreak, avoid constructing a solid,

A mesh fence like the one shown above is the most effective form of windbreak, if not the most attractive. It reduces buffeting yet lets a flow of fresh air through.

impermeable barrier. The moving air has to go somewhere; when it meets a solid barrier such as a brick wall it will be deflected up over the top of it, causing damaging downdraughts and eddies on the other side. The barrier itself will also be prone to being weakened or blown down. A semi-permeable barrier, on the other hand, will be much more effective at cutting down the wind speed and force. A hedge, 'hit-and-miss' fencing, trellis

Bush roses and other hedging plants will afford at least some protection to tender plants from wind when planted close together in rows, as here.

Individual plants can be given protection by

lightly clothed with plants or specially designed plastic windbreak netting are all suitable. Aim for around 50 per cent permeability for the best effect.

Give individual plants protection by constructing a temporary barrier on the windward side. You will find that two or three strong stakes, with sacking, plastic sheeting or windbreak netting tacked firmly across them, will usually provide susceptible plants with sufficient shelter. You can give extra protection to evergreens by spraying the foliage with an anti-transpirant spray which applies a harmless waxy coating to the leaves; this prevents them losing water and turning brown along the edges. This spray is often sold as a treatment for preventing needle-drop on Christmas trees indoors.

A yew hedge, though slow growing, is dense and compact, and so is ideal as a windbreak.

Rosa rugosa is a sturdy plant, well-suited to the high winds and tough conditions you might find near the seaside.

WINDBREAKS

The most effective form of windbreak is one that allows some of the air to get through, but at a reduced speed, whether it's a natural break such as a hedge, or a man-made one like the slatted fence on the left. A solid windbreak, like the wall shown on the right, is not as effective, as the air is forced up, and then pulled downwards, creating a fierce downdraught and potentially damaging turbulence for more tender plants on the other side.

Elaeagnus pungens 'Maculata', whose variegated foliage is very striking in winter, is an excellent wind resister.

constructing a good temporary barrier

The Winter GREENHOUSE

A greenhouse is the perfect place to shelter tender plants in winter, and to bring on seedlings for early sowing.

DEPENDING ON your preferences – and needs – you can choose between aluminium and timber frame; freestanding or lean-to models; glass to ground or with a brick or wooden base. A greenhouse will be a much more valuable gardening asset if you can keep it frost free during the winter, allowing frost-tender plants to overwinter safely and early sowings to be made. In really cold regions, this means using some form of heating. Paraffin heaters were once the most popular method, but they are inconvenient to use; they must be filled and lit whenever you guess that the temperature might fall to dangerous levels. Another disadvantage is that they give off a lot of water vapour as they burn; this may result in a humid atmosphere which often encourages plant diseases.

Electricity is by far the most convenient power source, and often turns out to have the most economical running costs, too, because electric heating can be thermostatically controlled. This means that fuel is not wasted if the night, in fact, turns out to be warmer than

To keep the greenhouse warm, line with bubble wrap, and use an electric heater if possible. Ventilate on very sunny days.

Most pot plants will not become chilled if the temperature in the greenhouse remains above 7°C (45°F); stand them in shallow trays filled with gravel for drainage. You will also be able to raise early bedding plants at this temperature.

forecast. Electric fan heaters can also provide a buoyant, airy atmosphere in the greenhouse, which is excellent for the health of the plants. Always have an electricity supply to the greenhouse professionally installed.

It is a good idea to keep a maximum/minimum thermometer in the greenhouse so that you can check the heating is working efficiently and keeping the temperature to the required level. Water plants sparingly, taking care not to splash water on to foliage, crowns, floor and staging unnecessarily. Remove all dead

The greenhouse temperature needs to be about 16°C (60°F) to keep tropical plants, and higher for most of them to flower.

Aluminium greenhouses can look a bit functional in a garden, but have the virtues of being cheaper, easy to install, and of being excellent transmitters of light. Louvred vents help to control ventilation, but these types of greenhouse don't retain heat, and temperature regulation is sometimes difficult.

A half-boarded lean-to takes up less space in the garden, but needs plenty of wall space. For ventilation, it must have windows that open. Wooden frames and brick or wooden walls up to the level of the staging will help retain heat, thus reducing your heating bills.

Agave americana (century plant) is a succulent, often with variegated leaves. It requires a minimum winter temperature of 10°C (50°F).

and dying foliage and flowers immediately they are seen, taking them out of the greenhouse for disposal; grey mould disease (botrytis) takes hold on dead plant material in a cool, moist atmosphere and will rapidly spread to healthy tissue.

Choosing a new greenhouse If you do not already have a greenhouse, winter is a good time to buy so that it is ready to use for the spring season. Obtain plenty of catalogues, browse through them carefully and take your time over the decision. Buy as large a greenhouse as you can afford, but also remember that you will need to bear in mind heating costs and maintenance.

You decision will depend on personal preference, space available in the garden, and what you intend to use the greenhouse for. Many companies offer an erection service and this should

For good air circulation, the greenhouse needs either skylights or a window that opens, and perhaps louvres around the base which can be opened in hot weather.

be seriously considered – putting up a greenhouse is always more difficult and time consuming than you at first think it is going to be.

Summer-blooming *Hibiscus rosa-sinensis* (rose of China) needs a winter rest at 16°C (60°F), to dry out its soil.

Frost-tender *Pavonia hastata* blooms in summer, and must be kept at a minimum of 16°C (60°F) to survive the winter indoors.

Buying Seeds FOR NEXT YEAR

Buying seeds for next year, and preparing everything you need to sow them, is one of the most fulfilling gardening tasks that you can undertake at this time of year.

Catalogues from the larger companies are usually well illustrated in colour, and often offer useful information on the habits and growing requirements of the different varieties. Most feature 'new' varieties, although these may only be new to the particular company that is selling them rather than true gardening novelties.

Prices of seeds vary widely; new varieties and F_1 hybrids are more expensive than older, open-pollinated types. The number of seeds in a packet is also very variable. Catalogues sometimes indicate the number of seeds per packet or, for vegetables, the length of row it should sow. The number of seeds may be as low as six for a particularly choice variety of new pelargonium, for instance, but more

Winter is the time to settle down with a good seed catalogue and plan a stunning garden for next year.

MOST GARDENERS find choosing the seeds to grow next year one of the most pleasurable gardening occupations. While garden shops and centres usually carry a reasonable range of seeds, mail order seed companies offer a much wider choice of varieties, and their catalogues make interesting reading for the winter evenings.

Seed packets from garden centres will satisfy the ambitions of most gardeners, but if you want to be a bit more adventurous, order from a seed catalogue.

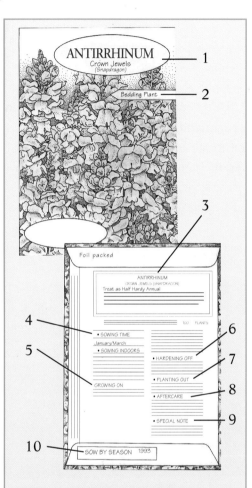

WHAT A SEED PACKET TELLS YOU

1 The scientific and common name of the plant.

2 The type of plant.

3 Description of the plant's growth habit and the soil it prefers.

4 The months or seasons in which to sow the seeds, the best method of sowing and information about suitable composts.

5 Instructions on pricking out.

6 How to prepare the seedlings for conditions outdoors.

7 When to transplant, and advice on spacing.

8 Plant care.

9 Special characteristics of the plant.

10 The last sowing date.

than 1000 for some of the small-seeded annuals such as alyssum or antirrhinum.

Before ordering your seeds, check that you will be able to supply them with the conditions they need; for some types, a heated propagator or greenhouse is necessary for good results. Many catalogues also offer young plants as well as seeds in a limited range of varieties, and these may be a more practical buy. A range of sizes is available, from tiny seedlings to young plants ready for potting on before planting. Although they are more expensive than seeds, they may turn out to be more economical in the long run.

Seed catalogues begin arriving in late autumn. If you want to be sure of getting all the seeds you want, especially if they include some of the new varieties, try to send your order off before midwinter. There is nearly always a last order date for young plants, and this date will vary from one variety to another, even from the same supplier. Remember that they may well be sold out if you leave it to the last minute.

Once the seeds arrive, store them in cool, dark, dry place until you are ready to sow them. If they are stored in a shed, make sure mice and slugs can't reach them; a tin or plastic box with a tight-fitting lid is ideal. Add a sachet of silica gel to help keep the seeds dry.

Quite large specimens of popular plants, such as fuchsias and pelargoniums, are usually potted up individually for growing on. Small seedlings are usually sold in trays.

Plug plants come in different sizes, and you will find them sold in lightweight plastic or polystyrene trays. They are easy to pull out of the tray and pop into larger containers for growing on.

Larger seedlings of annuals for planting out in the garden are often sold in trays or strips.

Sowing SEEDS INDOORS

Soak the large seeds of *Lathyrus odoratus* (sweet pea), or nick the hard coating, before sowing them indoors in order to bring them on well before planting out.

In order to germinate, seeds need warmth and moisture. A heated propagator will supply bottom heat to warm the compost, which also holds the moisture to enable the seed coat to soften and the seed to swell. While this bottom heat encourages even and rapid germination, most seeds will germinate without it, as long as they are kept in a moderately warm temperature.

A bright windowsill is an ideal place to keep seedlings and cuttings if you don't have a greenhouse.

If you can start off some of your seeds early, either indoors or in a greenhouse, you will have seedlings ready to plant out as soon as weather conditions allow.

THE TIME to start making some early sowings for the next season, to give you a head start on the weather, is mid- to late winter. In order to do this, you will need a heated greenhouse or conservatory, a heated propagator, or (at the very least) a warm, bright windowsill in the home. Not only must the seeds have sufficient warmth in which to germinate, but you must be able to provide suitable bright, warm conditions for the seedlings, which will take up much more space as they grow on. It is better to delay sowing for a little while than have a windowsill full of leggy, straggly seedlings with no place to go.

Once the seedling breaks through the compost surface, it needs light to keep it sturdy and compact. This should be bright, diffuse light – direct sunlight is too intense for young seedlings. Trays with plastic covers in the greenhouse can be shaded with a single sheet of newspaper; on a windowsill in the home, a net curtain or translucent blind works well. The seedlings should be gradually acclimatized to brighter conditions. In the greenhouse they will receive all-round light, but on a windowsill the light source is one-sided, and trays will have to be given a quarter-turn regularly to keep the seedlings growing straight. Remember, too, that on cold nights, windowsills can be very chilly places, several degrees colder than the rest of the room. Never pull the curtains across a deep windowsill, so cutting off trays of seeds or seedlings from the warmth of the room.

Many tender plants, often regarded just as house plants, will thrive outdoors. Sow the seeds indoors in winter or early spring.

A biennial usually treated as an annual, *Exacum affine* bears masses of tiny flowers in spring and summer.

**Seeds that benefit
from early sowing:**

Flowers
Begonia semperflorens
Coleus
Exacum
**Hardy and half-hardy
annuals**
Impatiens
Lathyrus
Pelargoniums
Solanum capsicastrum
Streptocarpus

Vegetables
Broad beans
Summer cabbage
Summer cauliflower
Lettuce
Onion
Spinach
Tomatoes

Sow the seeds of *Solanum capsicastrum* (false Jerusalem cherry) in late winter, and the plants will bear orange-red berries that remain all through the following winter.

Streptocarpus x hybridus 'Falling Stars' can be raised from seed sown in late winter or from leaf cuttings in spring and summer.

Step-by-Step SEED SOWING

Seeds can be sown in a seed tray, half-tray or pot, depending on the number of seeds to be raised, but the principles of sowing are the same in each instance.

An outdoor cold frame is ideal for bringing on reasonably hardy seedlings and protecting plants in winter.

1 Heap sowing and cutting or multi-purpose compost in the container, pushing it out well to the corners. Level off the compost with a wooden board, and firm it lightly with a presser. (Make one of these by cutting a piece of wood to fit the tray and nailing a handle to the centre.) Water the compost using a fine rose on the watering can, and leave the tray to

1   2   3

Remove the newspaper or seed tray cover

Lettuce seedlings need careful protection from slugs, snails and other garden pests as they grow to maturity.

drain for a short while before sowing.

2 Sow the seeds thinly and evenly over the surface of the compost, either by making a V-shaped crease in the edge of the seed packet and trickling the seeds through it, or by shaking the seeds carefully from the palm of your hand. Large seeds (such as sweet peas) can be spaced individually; very fine, dust-like seeds can be mixed with a little silver sand as a spreader (see right).

3 After sowing, cover all but very fine seeds with a layer of compost. Use a sieve in order to achieve an even covering of compost, or sift compost over the seeds by rubbing it between the palms of your hands. Some soilless composts are rather fibrous and lumpy, and in such a situation it is almost always easier to use vermiculite or sand as a covering material instead.

4 Cover the sown tray to keep the temperature and humidity constant. Use a plastic propagator cover, a sheet of glass topped with a double layer of newspaper, or an inverted seed tray. Remove the newspaper or seed tray cover as soon as the first seedlings appear, and remove the glass when the first seedling touches it. The propagator cover can remain in place for longer. Open vents, if fitted, to gradually increase the amount of air admitted. Prick out the seedlings into a tray or individual pots when they are large enough to handle comfortably, and do it before they become too crowded.

Fine or large seeds need different treatments for best results, and hard-coated seeds benefit either from being given a slight nick with a sharp knife on the side opposite the eye or being left to soak in a bowl of cold water for 12 hours.

Fine seeds can be a bit tricky to handle and measure accurately, so mix them with a small quantity of fine silver sand in a clean jar, and then scatter the mixture evenly over a tray of damp compost.

Sow large seeds by hand, spacing them about 2.5cm (1in) apart so that you don't have to prick them out too soon. Push the seeds into the compost, then gently water the tray.

4

as soon as the first seedlings appear

Bare-root TREES AND SHRUB

Bare-root trees and shrubs can be planted at almost any time in the dormant season, but once you have them they need to be put into the ground as soon as possible.

BARE-ROOT subjects (see page 112) can be planted at virtually any time during the dormant season. This is an ideal way to buy some of the more unusual specimens of trees and shrubs which are not available at garden centres, but have to be ordered from specialist nurseries. They will normally be delivered by carrier, with the roots wrapped in plastic, paper or sacking, at some time over the winter.

Because the roots will deteriorate the longer they are exposed to air and allowed to dry out, bare-root plants should be dealt with promptly on arrival. The packaging should be removed immediately, and any damaged portions of root trimmed off with secateurs. If the roots look dry, they should be soaked in a bucket of water for several hours. As long as the soil is not waterlogged or frozen, planting can

Nursery gardens often deliver bare-root trees with the roots and stem wrapped in straw, and with an outer covering such as paper, plastic sheet or sacking.

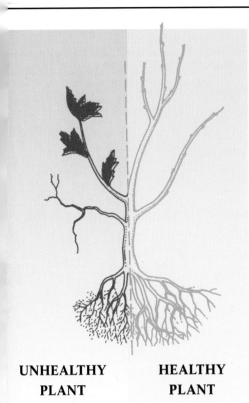

UNHEALTHY PLANT **HEALTHY PLANT**

BARE-ROOT PLANTS

Points to check: Is the root system well developed and spreading, or is it sparse and damaged? Are the stems healthy, or are some of them shrivelled? Is the plant starting to show signs of early budding when it ought to be dormant?

A good bare-root specimen such as this tree has a well-developed root system and, most importantly, the small, fine roots are not damaged. Make sure that the hole prepared for the tree is large enough to accommodate the roots without bending them, and take care to handle the plant gently when setting it in the hole.

take place immediately, following the procedure outlined on page 114. If it is not possible to plant straightaway, the roots can be re-covered with plastic or damp sacking for a few hours; keep the plant in a shed or a similar shelter out of cold, drying winds.

If planting has to be delayed for longer than a few hours, the plant should be heeled in to a spare piece of ground. This means digging a shallow trench and laying the tree or shrub in it at an angle so that all the roots can be covered with moist soil. Firm the soil into place lightly with the ball of your foot.

The reason for laying the tree or shrub at an angle is so that the stem is supported, and the plant is not subject to damaging wind rock. Once trees and shrubs have been heeled in, they can be safely left for several days, either until conditions improve or until it is a more convenient time to plant them. Don't let the soil covering the roots dry out.

If there is not a suitable area for heeling in a tree or shrub, place the roots in a strong plastic sack or container and fill it with potting compost, peat or soil.

Buying large trees in containers can be very expensive. It is much cheaper to buy them bare-rooted.

This young tree, *Cornus controversa* 'Variegata', is known as the wedding-cake tree because its branches grow in tiers.

An excellent specimen tree, *Davidia involucrata* (pocket handkerchief tree), with huge white bracts, originates in China.

Uncommon varieties such as this *Acer palmatum* 'Eddisbury' (Japanese maple) usually have to be ordered from nurseries.

Plants for WINGER (1)

Don't believe that the winter garden is a dull place – it has its own attractions and qualities that rival the garden in summer, from variegated leaves, colourful buds, berries and tree bark to winter blooms and fragrance.

The eye-catching bright red young stems of the dogwoods *Cornus alba* and the yellow-green stems of *C. Stolonifera*.

ALTHOUGH WE cannot hope to match the full glory of summer in the winter garden, it need by no means be a dull, dead season. There are plenty of plants to brighten the scene with foliage, flowers or just their winter outlines against a clear, cold sky.

Evergreens give form and structure to the garden all year round, but come into their own in winter, without competition from deciduous plants. Variegated or golden-leaved varieties provide sunshine even on cloudy days. *Euonymous fortunei* 'Emerald 'n' Gold' and *Elaeagnus pungens* 'Maculata' are two deservedly popular subjects with their brightly gold-splashed leaves; ivies, particularly the large-leaved

A hardy shrub, *Osmanthus burkwoodii* is good for hedging, since its leaves are a dark glossy green all year round; in spring it bears small, fragrant white flowers.

Hedera colchica 'Dentata Variegata', and hollies such as *Ilex* x *altaclerensis* 'Golden King' also make a good display. Berry-bearing plants – hollies, pyracantha, cotoneaster, berberis and skimmia, among others – provide splashes of colour until cold weather drives garden birds to feast on them, cutting the display short. Red berries are the first to go – orange and yellow-berried varieties tend to last longer.

There is a surprising number of flowers in winter, too, and the blooms often have the bonus of a strong scent. *Viburnum bodnantense* and *V. farreri*, *Chimonanthus fragrans*, *Mahonia*, *Lonicera fragrantissima*, *Daphne odora* and *Hamamelis* all have a wonderful fragrance. Other plants in flower include *Erica carnea* (winter-flowering heathers), *Jasminum nudiflorum* (winter jasmine), *Helleborus niger* (Christmas rose) and winter-flowering pansies, at their best in the early and late season. *Skimmia japonica* 'Rubella' does not open its flowers until spring, but the red-flushed buds make a very attractive winter feature.

Coloured bark and branches also make a valuable winter contribution. *Cornus alba* 'Sibirica'

There are plenty of plants to brighten the scene with flowers in winter

and *Salix alba* 'Britzensis' are grown as stooled shrubs for their red and orange young stems. Several maples have attractive bark and stems, including *Acer griseum*, *A. capillipes* and *A. davidii*; the white, peeling bark of birches shines out, as does the polished mahogany lustre of *Prunus serrula*. For a touch of eccentricity, few things can beat the contorted and twisted branches of *Salix babylonica pekinensis* 'Tortuosa' (Pekin willow), or *Corylus avellana* 'Contorta' (corkscrew hazel) – particularly attractive when hung with its winter catkins.

Below are just a few of the plants that lend style and character to the garden in winter.

The glossy leaves and attractive berries of *Berberis darwinii* stand out in winter, followed by attractive flowers in spring.

Clusters of purplish scented flowers appear on the hardy *Daphne retusa* towards the end of winter and throughout early spring.

Mahonia x 'Charity' produces large clusters of scented flower spikes in late winter, followed by blue-black berries.

Plants for WINTER (2)

Many gardeners tend to believe that winter is a season when most plants are dormant and visual interest in the garden will therefore be at an all-time low. However, this need not be the case.

IT IS POSSIBLE to create beauty and visual interest in the winter garden through a wide range of plants, with a variety of forms, colours and textures. These are some of the best for the entire season. All are widely available.

Euonymus fortunei 'Silver Queen' has broad green, white-edged leaves.

Early winter

Trees and shrubs

Acer capillipes,
   A. davidii,
   A. griseum
Aucuba japonica
   'Crotonifolia'
Betula
Chimonanthus

The bright red summer fruits of varieties of *Aucuba japonica* persist throughout the winter, cheering the dullest days.

   praecox
Cornus alba
Corylus avellana
   'Contorta'
Cotoneaster
Elaeagnus

Erica carnea
Euonymus fortunei,
   E. japonicus
   (variegated types)
Hamamelis mollis
Hedera colchica
   'Dentata Variegata'
   and others
Hippophae
   rhamnoides
Ilex (berry-bearing
   and variegated
   varieties)
Jasminum nudiflorum
Lonicera
   fragrantissima,
   L. standishii
Mahonia
Prunus serrula,
   P. x subhirtella
   'Autumnalis'
Pyracantha
Salix alba,
   S. babylonica
   pekinensis
   'Tortuosa'
Skimmia japonica
Sorbus
Viburnum

The curiously twisted branches of *Corylus avellana* 'Contorta' (corkscrew hazel) are most evident in winter.

Perennials

Helleborus niger
Iris unguicularis
Schizostylis coccinea
Viola (winter-
   flowering pansies)

Bulbs

Crocus imperati
Cyclamen coum
Galanthus

Midwinter

Trees and shrubs

Acer capillipes,

A. davidii,
   A. griseum
Aucuba japonica
   'Crotonifolia'
Betula
Chimonanthus
   praecox
Cornus alba
Corylus avellana
   'Contorta'
Cotoneaster
Daphne odora
Erica carnea
Euonymus fortunei,
   E. japonicus
   (variegated
   varieties)
Hamamelis mollis
Hedera colchica
   'Dentata Variegata'
   and others
Hippophae
   rhamnoides
Ilex (berry-bearing

Scented *Hamamelis mollis* (Chinese witch hazel).

Daphne odora 'Aureomarginata' bears fragrant purple flowers in late winter.

Long, grey-green catkins adorn the shrub *Garrya elliptica* in late winter.

The late winter months are full of colour, with many plants producing flowers as well as interesting foliage.

The cup-shaped flowers of *Helleborus orientalis* (Christmas rose) rise above the dense foliage in late winter on stems up to 40cm (18in) long.

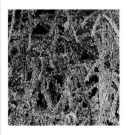

Good for ground cover or growing against a wall, *Cotoneaster horizontalis* keeps its berries almost the whole winter through.

Evergreen *Bergenia cordifolia* forms clumps of large crinkled leaves, and bears spikes of pink flowers in early spring.

and variegated types)
Jasminum nudiflorum
Lonicera
  fragrantissima,
  L. standishii
Mahonia
Prunus serrula,
  P. x *subhirtella*
  'Autumnalis'
Pyracantha
Salix alba,
  S. babylonica
  pekinensis
  'Tortuosa'
Skimmia japonica
Sorbus
Viburnum

Perennials
Ajuga reptans
Bergenia
Phormium tenax
Viola (winter-flowering pansies)

Bulbs
Crocus
Galanthus

Late winter
Trees and shrubs
Acer capillipes,
  A. davidii,
  A. griseum
Aucuba japonica
  'Crotonifolia'
Betula

The single *Narcissus* 'February Gold', with clear gold petals, blooms in late winter and is good for naturalizing.

Camellia
Chimonanthus
  praecox
Cornus alba
Corylus avellana
  'Contorta'
Cotoneaster
Erica carnea
Euonymus japonicus
  (variegated types)
Garrya elliptica
Hamamelis

Hedera colchica
  'Dentata Variegata'
  and others
Hippophae
  rhamnoides
Ilex (berry-bearing
  and variegated
  varieties)
Jasminum nudiflorum
Lonicera
  fragrantissima,
Mahonia
Prunus serrula,
Pyracantha
Salix alba,
  S. babylonica
  pekinensis
  'Tortuosa'
Sarcococca
  hookeriana,*Skimmia*
Sorbus
Stachyurus praecox
Viburnum

Perennials
Bergenia
Helleborus niger,
  H. orientalis
Phormium tenax

Bulbs
Anemone blanda
Chionodoxa
Crocus
Eranthis hyemalis
Galanthus
Narcissus

INDEX

ACKNOWLEDGEMENTS

If the publishers have unwittingly infringed copyright in any illustration reproduced, they would pay an appropriate fee on being satisfied to the owner's title.

t = top; b = bottom; l = left; r = right; c = centre

2 Focus Publishing; 5t/b Focus Publishing; 6t Jason Smalley/Wildscape, 6b Harry Smith Collection; 7t Focus Publishing, 7b Jacqui Dracup; 8 Focus Publishing; 9tl Focus Publishing; 10t Focus Publishing, 10bl Chas Wilder, 10tr Chas Wilder, 10/11 Andrew Lawson; 11tl Harry Smith Collection, 11tc Focus Publishing, 11tr Harry Smith Collection, 11c Chas Wilder; 12/13 Chas Wilder; 14/15 Chas Wilder; 16tl Andrew Lawson, 16tc Harry Smith Collection, 16tr Harry Smith Collection, 16br Harry Smith Collection, 16cl Andrew Lawson, 16bc Jacqui Dracup; 18bl Suttons Seeds, 18t Peter McHoy; 19t/b Suttons Seeds; 20 Jacqui Dracup; 22b Andrew Lawson, 22t Debi Wager/Garden Matters; 24/25 Chas Wilder; 26 Harry Smith Collection; 28 Focus Publishing; 30t Andrew Lawson, 30b Harry Smith Collection; 31l/r Adrian Weinbrecht; 32b Chas Wilder; 33l Suttons Seeds, 33tr Suttons Seeds, 33br Unwins Seeds Ltd; 34t Focus Publishing, 34b Steven Wooster; 35tr Focus Publishing, 35tc Focus Publishing, 35br Harry Smith Collection; 36/37 Harry Smith Collection; 38l Sheila Apps/Garden Matters; 40t Harry Smith Collection, 40l Dave Bevan; 41 Andrew Sydenham; 42 John Phipps/Garden Matters; 43 Garden Matters; 44 Adrian Weinbrecht; 45 Adrian Weinbrecht, 46 Harry Smith Collection; 47 Harry Smith Collection; 48 Steven Wooster; 49 Steven Wooster; 50tl Thompson & Morgan Ltd, 50/51 Peter Anderson; 51tl Garden Matters, 51tr Dave Bevan, 51cr Dave Bevan, 51br Dave Bevan; 52 Unwins Seeds Ltd; 53l Unwins Seeds Ltd, 53tr Andrew Lawson, 53br, Andrew Lawson, 53cr Harry Smith Collection; 54 Unwins Seeds Ltd; 56 Andrew Lawson; 57 Andrew Lawson; 58bl Garden Matters, 58c Wildlife Matters, 58br Garden Matters, 58t Andrew Lawson; 59tl Garden Matters, 59tr Harry Smith Collection 59c Harry Smith Collection, 59b Andrew Lawson; 60tl Focus Publishing, 60tc Focus Publishing, 60tr Focus Publishing, 60cr Focus Publishing, 60cl Focus Publishing, 60b Andrew Sydenham; 63tr Focus Publishing, 63br Focus Publishing, 63cr Harry Smith Collection; 64 Sutton Seeds; 65 Focus Publishing; 66 Sutton Seeds; 67 Adrian Weinbrecht; 68t Focus Publishing, 68bl Focus Publishing, 68br Chas Wilder; 69 Chas Wilder; 71 Focus Publishing; 72 Harry Smith Collection; 74b Peter Anderson, 74t Harry Smith Collection; 76 Focus Publishing; 77 Focus Publishing; 78l Andrew Lawson; 79 Unwins Seeds Ltd; 80l Garden Matters, 80/81t Chas Wilder; 81tr, 81cr, 81br Harry Smith Collection; 82 John Phipps/Garden Matters; 84 Focus Publishing; 86 Focus Publishing; 88l Focus Publishing, 88r Harry Smith Collection; 90 Chas Wilder; 91 Harry Smith Collection; 92/3 Harry Smith Collection; 94bl Focus Publishing,, 94/95 Focus Publishing; 96 Andrew Lawson/Eastgrove Cottage, Hereford; 98l Focus Publishing, 98r Unwins Seeds Ltd; 99l Thompson & Morgan, 99r Garden Matters; 100t Focus Publishing, 100b Sutton Seeds;101tl Sutton Seeds, 101tr Focus Publishing, 101b Sutton Seeds; 102l Sutton Seeds, 102t Unwins Seeds Ltd, 102b Unwins Seeds Ltd; 103t Sutton Seeds, 103b Sutton Seeds; 104tl Garden Matters, 104tc Ken Gibson/Garden Matters, 104tr Harry Smith Collection, 104cr Jason Smalley/Wildscape, 104b Jacqui Dracup, 104cl Andrew Lawson; 106t Garden Matters, 106b Peter Anderson; 107 Harry Smith Collection, 108l Harry Smith Collection; 108r Adrian Weinbrecht; 109tl/tc Adrian Weinbrecht, 108tr/b Steven Wooster; 110 Andrew Lawson; 111l Harry Smith Collection, 111r Steven Wooster; 112l Harry Smith Collection, 112r Focus Publishing; 114/115 Adrian Weinbrecht; 116 Harry Smith Collection; 117l Garden Matters, 117cr Garden Matters, 117tr Garden Matters, 117br Harry Smith Collection; 118l Focus Publishing, 118r Garden Matters, 118/119 Focus Publishing; 120t Harry Smith Collection, 120b Andrew Lawson; 121 Focus Publishing; 122t Harry Smith Collection, 122b Steven Wooster; 123bl Steven Wooster, 123tr Andrew Lawson, 123cr Andrew Lawson, 123br Jacqui Dracup; 124l Harry Smith Collection; 125tl Harry Smith Collection, 125tr Andrew Lawson, 125c Andrew Lawson, 125br Andrew Lawson; 126b Harry Smith Collection, 126t Garden Matters; 127 Suttons Seeds Ltd; 128l Chas Wilder; 129tr Chas Wilder, 129cr Harry Smith Collection, 129br Harry Smith Collection; 130 Andrew Lawson; 131t Harry Smith Collection; 132t Focus Publishing, 132b Peter Anderson; 133 Dave Bevan; 134l Colin Milkins/Garden Matters, 134c Dave Bevan; 136 Amateur Gardening Magazine; 137 Harry Smith Collection; 138 Wildlife Matters; 139 Debi Wager Stock Pictures/Garden Matters; 140 Jason Smalley/Wildscape; 142 S.North/Garden Matters, 142/143 Harry Smith Collection; 144 Jacqui Dracup; 145 Harry Smith Collection; 146l Harry Smith Collection, 146c Andrew Lawson, 146r Andrew Lawson; 147t Garden Matters, 147b Harry Smith Collection; 148tl Jaqui Dracup, 148tc Harry Smith Collection, 148cl Harry Smith Collection, 148cr Jacqui Dracup 148tr Andrew Lawson, 148b Jacqui Dracup; 150 Harry Smith Collection; 151tr Jacqui Dracup; 152 Amateur Gardening; 154b Chas Wilder, 154t Focus Publishing; 155 Chas Wilder; 156 Peter Anderson; 158/159 Andrew Lawson; 162 Paskett PR; 163t Amateur Gardening, 163bl Amateur Gardening, 163br Paskett PR; 164 Andrew Lawson; 165 Harry Smith Collection; 166bl Harry Smith Collection, 166t Andrew Lawson; 168l Peter Anderson, 168/169 Harry Smith Collection; 169tr Brogdale Slide Library, 169c Brogdale Slide Library,, 169br Brogdale Slide Library; 170 Peter McHoy; 172 Andrew Lawson; 173t Garden Matters, 173c Andrew Lawson, 173b Wildlife Matters; 174l Focus Publishing, 174/175 Harry Smith Collection; 175l Harry Smith Collection, 175r Focus Publishing; 176 Harry Smith Collection; 177r Focus Publishing; 178t John Glover, 178br Chas Wilder; 179r Chas Wilder; 180t Andrew Lawson, 180/181 Holt Studios International, 181r Chas Wilder; 182t Harry Smith Collection; 183t John Glover; 184 Harry Smith Collection; 185r Focus Publishing; 186 Harry Smith Collection; 187 Jacqui Dracup; 188l Harry Smith Collection, 188t Andrew Lawson, 188c Harry Smith Collection 188b Jacqui Dracup; 189tl Andrew Lawson, 189tc Jacqui Dracup, 189bl/br Andrew Lawson, Jacqui Dracup, 189c John Phipps/Garden Matters.

Illustrators
Patricia Capon, Lynn Chadwick, Jim Channell, Karen Gavin, Will Giles, Kuo Kangchen, Stuart Lafforde, Coral Mula, Kate Osborne, Liz Pepperel, Sandra Pond, Jim Robins, Gill Tomblin, John Woodcock, Ann Winterbotham.